A Prayer Journal for Today's Seeker

The Many Faces of God

Dennis R. Keller

AVE MARIA PRESS   Notre Dame, Indiana 46556

© 1991 by Ave Maria Press, Notre Dame, IN 46556

International Standard Book Number: 0-87793-462-2

Library of Congress Catalog Card Number: 91-72116

Cover and text design by Elizabeth J. French

Illustrations by Sarah Smiley

Printed and bound in the United States of America.

To my wife, Betsy
and our daughters, Jennifer and Rachel
loving companions in my journey toward knowing God

Contents

Introduction

One morning our daughter Rachel, not quite a year old at the time, awoke us at 5:30. After several unsuccessful attempts at trying to get her to go back to sleep, I agreed to take her into our living room and watch her while she played with some toys. For over an hour I sat in the quiet of the early morning and observed her at play. Her play time was a never-ending process of experiencing one toy, then another, approaching each one with a sense of curiosity and wonder. She would pick up a toy and look at it as she moved it around in her hands. She would try to pull it apart or push it together, or she would shake it to see if it made any noise. Often she would put toys in her mouth, as if wanting to experience them in every way. But she did not stay with any one toy for very long. After a short time with one toy she would notice another one and begin to explore it. Sometimes, upon making a new discovery, she would look in my direction and laugh. Rachel explored the world around her with joy and delight, totally absorbed in her experience of each toy.

As you begin this prayer experience, I invite you to reflect upon the image of a toddler playing with toys. I will use this image as a way of introducing this workbook to you. I believe we can learn something about prayer by watching toddlers play.

A Special Time and Place

Toddlers at play teach us, first of all, that if we are to be attentive to God in prayer we need to set apart a time and a place without noise or distractions. Toddlers have no concern for time when they play. They are simply absorbed in the present moment with the objects of their play. They are not occupied, as we often are, with the need to do many things or to be certain places at certain times. Their play is leisurely and relaxed. It is important for us to set aside such leisurely, relaxed time for our prayer.

In his book *True Prayer*, Kenneth Leech suggests that we can discover more fully the meaning of prayer by looking at our human experiences of relating to others.[1] One thing important to healthy human relationships is for those involved in them to spend time together. Imagine how exasperating it would be to try to relate to someone who wanted nothing to do with you most of the time, but when a problem arose or a need came up, that person expected you to respond immediately. Such a relationship could cause us much stress, especially if it were with someone about whom we care very deeply.

Growth in our relationship with God takes place in much the same way as growth in our human relationships. Our relationship with God is hindered when we turn to God only when we are in trouble or when we need something. If we pay no attention to God most of the time, if we turn to God only during a few brief troubled moments, we cannot expect to be able to discern the caring presence of our closest companion.

Anthony Bloom writes of the importance of setting apart time to be attentive to our relationship with God in prayer:

> If you look at the relationship [with God] in terms of mutual relationship, you will see that God could complain about us a great deal more than we about [God]. We complain that [God] does not make [Godself] present to us for the few minutes we reserve for [God], but what about the twenty-three and a half hours during which God may be knocking at the door and we answer "I am busy, I am sorry" or when we do not answer at all because we do not even hear the knock at the door of our heart, of our minds, of our conscience, of our life.[2]

Our relationship with God, like our human relationships, requires a commitment of time. But there is at least one important difference between our relationship with

God and our relationships with others. While it is possible for us to be with others only during certain periods of time, God is always with us. In other words, there is nowhere we can go that we are not in the presence of God. The Psalmist expresses it beautifully:

> Whither shall I go from thy Spirit?
>   Or whither shall I flee from thy
>   presence?
> If I ascend to heaven, thou art there!
>   If I make my bed in Sheol, thou
>   art there!
> If I take the wings of the morning
>   and dwell in the uttermost parts of
>   the sea,
> even there thy hand shall lead me,
>   and thy right hand shall hold me.
> — Psalm 139:7–10

The goal of prayer is not to "invoke" God's presence, as if we are trying to invite one who is absent from us to come and be with us. It is rather to recognize the presence of God who is always near us. To pray is to be attentive to how God is being revealed in every facet of our lives. While we can be attentive to God's work in us and in our world in the midst of everyday activities, it is important for us to set apart more focused times of prayer when we can direct our attention completely toward God.

During the next six weeks, as you use this workbook, you will be invited to set apart thirty minutes a day, and go to a quiet place where you can direct your attention toward God. It may be helpful to you, in keeping this discipline of prayer, to try to set aside a particular time and place each day for using the workbook. You may want to determine in advance that there will be nothing else for you to do during this time, in this place, but to be attentive to God. That way like the toddler who is attentive to only the objects of his or her play, you will be able to relax in the presence of God without distraction. When we try to squeeze prayer time into days already filled with activity, or try to tack it on at the end of a tiring day, it may be difficult for us to be open to God's presence. Consistent, daily time for prayer will help us to be attentive to God not only during our prayer time, but in all facets of our lives.

Prayer Involves Listening and Responding

Watching toddlers play reminds us that prayer involves not only talking but listening. Toddlers grow as they are open and responsive to the vast, mysterious world around them. As they look, and touch, and listen, and taste, and smell, they gradually discover their world and learn to relate to it. In the same way, as you and I are open and responsive to God's activity in our lives, we discover our world and its Creator, and we learn to relate in loving ways toward God, our neighbors, and ourselves.

Our prayer time can be an important part of this process of discovering God and learning to love. Usually we think of prayer as "talking to God." When we ask someone to pray before a meal or at a church meeting we expect that he or she will express the prayer verbally to God. Likewise, when we teach children to pray, we encourage them to "say their prayers." While putting our prayers of thanksgiving or sorrow or petition into words has a central place in prayer, in this workbook you will be invited to experience prayer as more than words or thoughts directed from us to God. Prayer is not just a one-way venture in which we talk and God listens. It involves listening on our part, being attentive to how God is being revealed to us.

Recalling what Kenneth Leech said about human relationships teaching us about our relationship with God, consider another type of potentially frustrating human encounter. Imagine how difficult it would be to try to relate to a friend who talked to you constantly, but was never interested in anything you had to say. Unless you had agreed in advance that this would be the nature of your relationship, the time you spend with this friend could be very draining. In fact, over time, you may feel that this person is not really interested in you at all, but is just using you to air his or her concerns. Eventually, you even may choose to avoid this person, not wanting to be "dumped on" again.

Healthy friendships are not one-sided affairs where one person uses another to meet certain desires or needs. Those that are most meaningful and joyous involve both giving and receiving. People grow in their love for one another as they relate mutually, sometimes talking, at other times listening. We grow in our love for God, and in the assurance of God's love for us, through such a mutual relationship with our divine companion. It can be refreshing for us to pour out our needs before our God who is always willing to listen to us. But if we are to experience more fully the loving concern and the gentle guidance God offers us, our prayer needs to include silence and attentiveness to how God is becoming present in our lives. In his book *Seeking the Face of God*, William H. Shannon reminds us that listening is a primary goal of prayer:

> To become aware of God's presence is to become aware of what is always there. We are always in God. We are not always aware that we are in God.... The chief purpose of prayer is to achieve and to deepen that awareness.[3]

This workbook can assist you in deepening your awareness of how God is present in your life and in the world. You will be invited not only to be open to God but also to respond to God.

The Bible: Resource for Openness and Response

You will be asked to use the Bible as a primary resource during your prayer time. The Bible contains many different kinds of writings, spanning hundreds of years. Yet, there are at least two common threads running throughout its pages. First, while they did it in different ways, every biblical writer tried to put into words how they perceived God to be present in their lives, in their community, and in the world. Secondly, they tried to convey how God's people responded, or failed to respond, to God and what happened as a result.

It becomes apparent as we read the scriptures that the biblical writers were not satisfied simply to use a few words to talk about their experiences of God. For them, no words could contain God fully, so they used a variety of words. Another way of referring to these God-words is to call them "metaphors." A helpful definition of a metaphor is given by Sallie McFague.

> A metaphor is seeing one thing as something
> else, pretending "this" is "that" because we do
> not know how to think or talk about "this" so
> we use "that" as a way of saying something
> about it.[4]

No human words can describe God fully. Hence, the biblical writers used metaphors to talk about God. They used words that described things with which their hearers would be familiar to express their experiences of the Holy One who is beyond human description.

Often these metaphors for God were drawn from ordinary, everyday life. The writers of scripture drew from their experiences as mothers and fathers and children, and from their occupations, to talk about how God was present with them. They looked to nature, to the world of birds, animals, and other living things, to convey their experiences of God. In addition, they borrowed words from philosophy and the sciences to articulate how God had been revealed to them. Knowing that no words could describe God completely, the biblical writers used a vast number of words for God.

As you use this workbook, you will be invited to explore a variety of metaphors for God from the Bible. As a way of looking at how to explore these metaphors, recall again the image of Rachel playing with her toys — a particular toy would catch her eye, she would pick it up and explore it. Trying to experience how the toy felt, she would move it around in her hands, pulling it apart or pushing it together. Sometimes she would bring the object to her mouth or shake it to see if it rattled. She was not afraid to experiment, to see what would happen. Rachel didn't seem to give much thought to what she did; she was simply absorbed in each toy. Each one was a new adventure to be explored.

Like a parent scatters toys around a living room for a toddler, so the biblical writers have scattered before us many metaphors for God, inviting us to explore them as ways to experience God. You will be asked to do this by using a style of prayer that involves four stages. As you move through these stages in your daily prayer time, you will be invited to observe how God is being revealed to you, to listen for the voice of the gentle Shepherd, to feel the presence of the one who is closer to you than the air you breathe, and to "taste and see that the Lord is good" (Ps 34:8a). During your prayer time, you also will be encouraged to respond to God's presence. Your response may be offered in words expressed to God, or it may involve you in some act of service. The purpose of prayer is not just to make us feel good. It is to help us to be more loving in the way we relate to God, our neighbors, and ourselves. This workbook is intended to help you in your prayer life and, thereby, to facilitate your continuing growth in love.

Four Stages of Prayer

Each day, during the thirty minutes you have set aside, you will be asked to explore a particular metaphor for God. You will be guided in your explorations by participating in a style of prayer called *lectio divina* or "spiritual reading."[5] *Lectio divina*, which has its origins in Judaism from the sixth century B.C. and has been used widely in the Christian church since the first century A.D., has four stages: *lectio* (reading), *meditatio* (meditation), *oratio* (responding to God's address to us), and *contemplatio* (contemplation).

Stage One: Reading

The first thing to do, as you start your prayer time each day, is to spend a few moments in silence. The purpose of beginning with silence is to help you turn your attention away from the many daily affairs and focus upon God. Having a designated time and place for your prayer will help you in this process. During this initial silent time your goal will be to become still and relaxed, so that you may be open to God's presence with you.

When you feel that you have begun to be still in the silence with God, you will be asked to read a scripture passage that relates to a particular metaphor for God. Keep in mind that "spiritual reading" is different from the reading most of us are accustomed to doing. In his book *Shaped by the Word*, M. Robert Mulholland, Jr. makes a helpful contrast between "reading for information," and "reading for formation."[6] Most of the time we read for information. Ordinarily when we read, we seek to master a body of material that can be used by us for a certain purpose. An example of this type of reading is the way we read the newspaper. Usually we read articles in a newspaper rather quickly, taking in certain bits of information that will help us to be informed. In general, we have this same goal for magazine articles, novels, and most other kinds of reading.

Reading for formation takes place quite differently. The concern of this type of reading is not just to gather information. It is to listen for how God is being revealed to us as we read. When we read in openness to God we read slowly, as if we are eating a favorite food and we want to take in every bit of it, leaving no morsels on our plate. Some devotional writers suggest that our spiritual reading be done aloud, so that we not only may see the words with our eyes but may hear them address our ears as well. When we read with an eye toward being formed by God, we may spend a long time with a single verse of scripture or with one sentence of a devotional book. We may read just a few words several times, listening for the Word that is being revealed to us from God.

As you read the scripture passages during each day's prayer time, you are invited to "read for formation." Read slowly, and with an openness to God.

Stage Two: Meditation
It is not easy to distinguish when reading stops and meditation begins, for the first seems to move us naturally into the second. If, as we have seen above, spiritual reading can be compared to taking food into our mouths, then meditation may be likened to chewing the food. Having been introduced to a particular metaphor for God through your reading of scripture, you will be asked to begin now to explore how it relates to your own life.

Sometimes the truth upon which we ruminate is comforting to us. At other times it confronts us with a challenge. Mulholland uses the food metaphor to describe various ways God's address may affect us. He writes:

> Some of God's address may be sweet and we
> relish its refreshing savor. Some may be bit-
> ter and we will be tempted to reject it. Some
> may be tough to chew and we may be tempted
> to set it aside. Some may be like sand in our
> mouth and we want only to be rid of it.[7]

As you meditate upon the various metaphors for God, you will find some of them to be familiar and comfortable to you. But you may find that others will be new, and that still others may be quite disconcerting. Some of the metaphors may even make you angry. It may be difficult for you to think about God in certain ways. Whatever feelings you find arising during your prayer time, try not to dismiss any of the metaphors too quickly. Be especially attentive to the ones that seem bitter to you or tough to chew, for God can use all of our emotions, including our "negative" ones, to guide us in our spiritual journeys.

The workbook will offer some guidance for your meditation on each of the biblical metaphors. Brief reflections on the scripture reading for the day, along with questions, will help you relate the word to your own life.

Stage Three: "Oratio"

In your reading and meditation you are invited to be open to God addressing you through the scriptures. In this stage you will be asked to respond to how God has been revealed to you during the first two stages. *Oratio*, or response, means more than just "saying prayers." Part of what you will be guided to do at this stage will include offering words of thanksgiving or sorrow or petition to God. But, in addition to this, you will be challenged to respond in other ways. For example, having seen some aspect of yourself that you feel God is calling you to change, you may wish to determine at this stage how you will make that change. Or, seeing some need in your church or in the world, you may feel challenged to do something about it. Again, keep in mind that the end toward which prayer is directed is greater love for God, others, and ourselves. At this stage of prayer we are invited to explore how we will respond to God's love for us.

Stage Four: Contemplation

Your prayer time will have begun in silence. Now, as you come to the last stage of prayer, you will be invited to wait again in stillness before God. The waiting that takes place during "contemplation" is not just sitting passively by in quietness. Much will take place during this time. To contemplate is to observe what God is revealing to you in your prayer time and in your life as a whole. At this stage you will be asked to reflect upon how God has been present with you during the previous three stages. You also will be encouraged to be attentive to God's movement in your life beyond the specific time and place of your prayer. Each day's prayer experience will end with the invitation for you to yield yourself wholly to God, so that what is revealed to you during *lectio divina* will flow over into the rest of your life.

An Invitation

You are invited during the next six weeks to participate in a journey of scriptural prayer. Some of you may have been setting aside a time and a place for prayer for many years, and this workbook will be another resource for your prayer life. Others may be just beginning on the exciting journey of being open and responsive to God in an intentional way each day. Wherever you are in your prayer life, I pray that your use of this workbook will help you to move toward the true goal of every human life. Jesus summarized that goal when he responded to the question about the first of all commandments:

> "The first is, 'Hear, O Israel: The Lord our
> God, the Lord is one; and you shall love the
> Lord your God with all your heart, and with all
> your soul, and with all your mind, and with all
> your strength.' The second is this, 'You shall
> love your neighbor as yourself.' There is no
> other commandment greater than these" (Mk
> 12:29–31).

If this workbook enables you to move toward the goal of relating in more loving ways toward God, your neighbors, and yourself, its purpose will have been accomplished.

Notes

1 Kenneth Leech, *True Prayer: An Introduction to Christian Spirituality* (London: Sheldon Press, 1980), p. 4.

2 Anthony Bloom, *Beginning to Pray* (New York: Paulist Press, 1970), p. 26.

3 William H. Shannon, *Seeking the Face of God* (New York: Crossroad Publishing Company, 1988), p. 12.

4 Sallie McFague, *Metaphorical Theology: Models of God in Religious Language* (Philadelphia: Fortress Press, 1982), p. 15.

5 In describing the process of *lectio divina* I have drawn upon several resources: Anthony de Mello, *Sadhana: A Way to God* (St. Louis: The Institute of Jesuit Resources, 1978), pp. 101–105; Chester P. Michael and Marie C. Norrisey, *Prayer and Temperament: Different Prayer Forms For Different Personality Types* (Charlottesville, VA: The Open Door, Inc., 1984), pp. 31–45; M. Robert Mulholland, Jr.,

"Spiritual Reading of Scripture," in *Weavings* 3 (November/December, 1988), pp. 26–32; Shannon, *op. cit.*

6 M. Robert Mulholland, Jr., *Shaped by the Word: The Power of Scripture in Spiritual Formation* (Nashville: The Upper Room, 1985), pp. 47–60.

7 Mulholland, "Spiritual Reading of Scripture," p. 30.

WEEK ONE

Parental Metaphors: God as Father

Week 1, Day 1:

Being Open to God

Set apart thirty minutes today. Go to a quiet place and reread the introduction. Read it slowly, being open to what God may reveal to you in these pages. As you read, make notes in the margins and/or in the space provided here:

When you have finished reading and making notes, spend a few moments answering the following questions:

1.   Describe your prayer life at the present time. What persons, resources, and experiences have been most helpful to you in your life of prayer? What have been the greatest obstacles to prayer for you?

2. Perhaps it would be helpful for you at the outset of
this journey to determine a certain time and place you
would like to set apart for prayer. If you would find this
helpful, designate a particular time and place for prayer.

When you are finished reading and responding to
what you have read, spend a few moments in silence, being aware of God's love for you. Ask God to guide you as
you begin this journey in prayer.

Week 1, Day 2:

God Our Father Desires Our Companionship

Reading: Spend a few moments in silence, becoming
aware of the presence of God, who desires your companionship during this time of prayer. Read Matthew 6:5–15.

Meditation: During this week you will be invited to focus upon the metaphor of God as Father. As we can see in
our scripture text for today, and elsewhere in the gospels,
Jesus often called God "Father" and encouraged his followers to do so. For a majority of Christians, "father" is
one of the most familiar and most frequently used ways of
addressing God in prayer. Many find it to be a meaningful
way of expressing the kind of relationship they have experienced with God. And yet, this word raises a concern

for some Christians today. Like other words and phrases
that we use frequently in our daily conversations, "Father"
may become just an "empty phrase" (v 7), or one that conjures up negative images. When we address God in this
way, we may do it out of habit, without thinking about
what we really are saying when we call God Father.

Today you are invited to reflect upon what it means
for you to address God as Father. Jesus' use of this metaphor in prayer was not based upon some ritualistic phrase
he was taught to use when he prayed. His address to God
as Father flowed out of his life with God. "Father" expressed the deep and intimate relationship Jesus felt with
God. As a child experiences loving companionship with
a caring and supportive father, so God seeks to relate to
us. In prayer we are invited to be open and responsive to
the Father who desires such an intimate relationship with
us. Take a few moments now to meditate upon the following questions as you consider your relationship with "Our
Father."

1.   What do you learn from today's scripture reading
about God our Father?

2.   How have you experienced companionship with God
in your life? What was/is that like for you?

3. In there anything in your life at the present time that may be keeping you from having the kind of intimate companionship you believe God desires with you?

Response: Give thanks for God's relationship with you.

Express sorrow for how you may have hindered that relationship.

Ask God to help you to be receptive to his companionship with you as you are involved in the activities of this day.

During the day today, receive the promise of these words: "Those who are led by God's Spirit are God's [children]. For the Spirit that God has given you does not make you slaves and cause you to be afraid; instead, the Spirit makes you God's children, and by the Spirit's power we cry out to God, 'Father! my Father!'" (Rom 8:14–15 Good News Bible).

Contemplation: As you come to the end of your prayer time today, return again to silence, and be open to how God has been revealed to you during this time.

Week 1, Day 3:

God Our Father Cares for Us

Reading: Following a few moments of silence, focusing on God's presence with you as you begin your prayer time, read Matthew 6:25–33.

Meditation: Observe the four characters in this passage.

First, there are "the birds of the air" (v 26). Their lives are marked by simplicity. It is enough for them simply to exist. God the Father supplies them with all they need: voices to sing, twigs to build their nests, food for their young, and wings to soar. Receiving their small provision from God, and using it to care for themselves and the other birds in their nest, they glorify their Creator.

Second, notice "the lilies of the field" (v 28–29). Lilies do not grow by the strain of their own efforts. In openness to the moisture and nutrition they receive from the soil around them, they become strong and blossom and glorify God with the splendor of their beauty.

The third character is humanity. Jesus describes us as an anxious lot. Our lives are depicted as continual struggles to be productive. We are not satisfied, as the birds are, to accept a few basic necessities for ourselves and to share the rest with others. We want to be secure, to have "stored away" enough so that we can always have an abundance of many things. Nor is it enough for us to be like the lilies: to live in constant openness to the Father who would nurture us and give us true beauty. It is difficult for us to order our lives so that such openness can become a possibility. We are busy filling our schedules with more important things that will help us to become "successful" or to receive the adoring gaze of others. Much that troubles people today results from their misplaced trust in "earthly treasures."

Look now at the Father, the fourth character in this text. God cares for us and for all creation. God provides for the birds, and adorns the lilies. How much more is God concerned for you and me! What a difference it would make in our lives if we could be more aware of the Father's care for us and live more simply. An important invitation in this passage is this: Trust in God. Reflect upon how you would like to respond to this invitation as you answer these questions:

1. As you think about your life at the present time, what are you anxious about? What are the consequences of worrying for you?

2. Was there ever a time when you became vividly aware of God's care for you? If so, what was that awareness like for you? If not, what do you think that would be like for you?

3.   What difference would it make in your life to "seek
first God's kingdom"?

Response: Let your verbal prayers to God flow out of
how you feel God has been moving in your life during
this time. Here are a few possibilities:

Praise God for God's care for you.
Be sorry for the times when you have not trusted in
the Father's care.
Ask God to help you with a certain need you are anxious about. Be assured that your Father in heaven
hears your prayers and will respond to them.

Repeat these words several times throughout the day
today: "But seek first God's kingdom and God's righteousness, and all these things will be yours as well." Consider,
as you recall this verse, what changes God may be challenging you to make in order to be more trusting in God's
care.

Contemplation: End your prayer time in silence, aware of
how God has been present with you.

Week 1, Day 4:

God Our Father Is Faithful Amid Troubles

Reading: Begin your time of prayer today, as you are invited to begin each prayer time, in silence. Then read Mark 14:32–42.

Meditation: As you reflect upon this passage, consider these words by hymn writer William B. Tappan as he recalls this darkest night in the life of Jesus:

Tis midnight, and on Olive's brow
The star is dimmed that lately shone;
Tis midnight, in the garden now
The suffering Savior prays alone.

Tis midnight, and from all removed,
The Savior wrestles lone with fears;
E'en that disciple whom he loved
Heeds not his Master's grief and tears.

It was surely midnight in Jesus' life. Abandoned by even his most beloved disciples, he struggled in the garden alone. Soon to face betrayal by one of the Twelve, the scorn of his own people, the agony of a torturous beating, and the torment of death on a cross, Jesus was "very sorrowful, even to death" (v 34).

1.   Can you remember a time when you had a troubling "midnight" experience? What was that like for you?

2.   Are there any troubles confronting you at the present time? Explain.

Return again to the hymn:

Tis midnight, and for others' guilt
The Man of Sorrows weeps in blood;
Yet he that hath in anguish knelt
Is not forsaken by his God.

Tis midnight, and from heavenly plains
Is borne the song that angels know;
Unheard by mortals are the strains
That sweetly soothe the Savior's woe.

Jesus had been abandoned by his sleepy friends in the midnight of his life, but he was not alone. Amid his anguish he prayed, "Abba, Father." Some scholars translate the word *Abba* as "Daddy." As Jesus addressed God in this way, he looked to his Father as one with whom he had a most intimate relationship. God is not some distant father who stands afar off and is unaffected by our troubles. When children are afraid, or lonely, or hurt, they often find consolation in the arms of a caring daddy or mommy. In the same way God is present to soothe our woes when we are troubled.

3.   Return to the experience you described in your answer to question #1 above. Were you aware of the presence of God during that troubling time? If so, what was that like for you? If not, what may have prevented you from being aware of God's presence?

4. In question #2 above you were asked to reflect upon something that may be troubling you now. How do you see God being revealed to you in that troubling situation?

Response: In your vocal prayers today:

Remember with thanks that God, the Father, has been near to you throughout your life, in times of joy and in times of trouble. Ask for the grace to be aware of God's presence in your life now. Pray for others who are troubled in your own community and in the world.

Is there someone in your life who needs to be reminded that you care? Do something today to show them you care. Remember that God's care often is revealed in the way we relate to one another.

Contemplation: In silence, consider what God has revealed to you in your time of prayer.

Week 1, Day 5:

God Our Father Gives Us Freedom to Fail

Reading: Relax as you return again to this time and place that should be becoming familiar to you. Following the silence, read Luke 15:11–19.

Meditation: God our Father loves us and desires to relate to us. This is evident in the way God is present throughout our lives. But God does not coerce us into a relationship. No matter how much parents try to love their children, they never can force their children to love them in return. Love, if it is to be a true commitment of one person to another, must be given freely. As much as our Father desires our love, God did not create us so that we would have to love God in return. God comforts us, cajoles us, challenges us, and supports us. But God does not tie strings around us like some divine puppeteer and control us so that we are forced to love God. When it comes down to it, the choice is ours either to love God or to turn from God.

It was no easy thing for God to give us such freedom. We may abuse our freedom and make unwise choices. We may make choices that bring pain to God, to others, and to ourselves. In the church we have called such poor choices sins. Sin results in brokenness between God and us and division between our neighbors and ourselves. Observe in the first part of this familiar parable how the father gave his son the freedom to fail. Notice, too, the consequences faced by the son because he abused that freedom.

As we begin to look at how the son chose to wander away from his father and to squander his inheritance, we realize that we, too, have been prodigals. In a variety of ways we have sinned. Often, in worship, when we pray a prayer of contrition, we admit to being "sinners" in a general way. But this is not enough if we are to make progress in our journey toward becoming more loving in our relationships with God and God's children everywhere. It is important for us to be specific in identifying our sins so that we may turn from them.

1. Being as specific as you can, try to identify one or two ways that you have been unloving in your relationships with God, your neighbors, or yourself. Write them in the space below. (Remember that you do not have to share what you write in this workbook with anyone unless you choose to do so. What you write here is between you and God.)

2. Mindful of your sin, reflect now upon its consequences. What has happened or could happen to impoverish your life or the lives of others as a result of these unwise choices?

3.   Tomorrow you will be invited to focus upon God's
forgiving love. But perhaps now, even as you identify one
or two specific sins and their consequences, you feel some
release from their burden upon you. Write here what has
been revealed to you about God and about yourself during your prayer time today.

Response: Confess your sins to God.

Be assured that God, your Father, loves and forgives
you.
Commit yourself to turning from any particular sins
you have become most conscious of during your
prayer time, inviting God to help you.

During the day today, as you find a moment or two
between your various activities, recall these words: "If we
claim to be without sin, we deceive ourselves, and the
truth is not in us. If we confess our sins, God is faithful and just and will forgive us our sins and purify us
from all unrighteousness" (I Jn 1:8–9 New International
Version). Be open to how your awareness of these words
affects your relationships today.

Contemplation: As you come to the end of this time of prayer, return to a few moments of silence, and be aware of God's forgiving presence with you.

Week 1, Day 6:

God Our Father Loves Us Extravagantly

Reading: After your usual time of silence, read Luke 15:20–24.

Meditation: The father's heart must have been broken. He had given his young son the freedom to do whatever he wished with his share of the inheritance, and the son squandered it. As we observed yesterday, our heavenly Father gives us freedom. Sometimes we make poor choices. When we sin, we disappoint and frustrate and grieve God. But although we sometimes turn from God, God never turns from us.

This parable reminds us that the love of God our Father is long-suffering and extravagant. Consider the father in this story. Notice, first of all, that he never gave up on his wayward son. He must have been watching constantly, longing for the prodigal to return, because he saw his son while he was yet at a distance. And what the father did next was a surprise. After all this wayward son had put him through, the father may have returned to the house and refused even to see his son. But there seem to be no limits to this father's love. All that had happened in the past is forgotten. The father "ran and embraced him and kissed him" (v 20). Without hesitation he leaped up and tenderly welcomed his weary son.

In the same way, observe how extravagantly this father loved his repentant son. He didn't greet his son with some quiet, "Nice to see you again, son." He lavishly welcomed him home, giving him the best of everything: the best robe, a fine ring, new shoes, and a great feast! Such extravagance seems to us to be unfair. This son deserves punishment, not reward. Perhaps making him a servant would have been a fairer welcome for him (see v 25–31). But this father welcomed his son with exuberant joy as he exclaimed: "This my son was dead and is alive again; he was lost, and is found" (v 24).

1.   How does it make you feel that God, your Father, relates to you with the same kind of long-suffering, extravagant love that the father in this parable had toward his son? List your feelings here.

2.   What difference would it make in your life if you would love with the extravagance of God? What difference would it make in your church and in the world?

Response: As you pray today, be aware that when you turn to God, God is always ready to receive your prayers. You may wish to pray for particular relationships with family members, friends, and others whom you feel called to pray for during this time. Ask God to help you to be more loving in the way you relate to those around you today.

During the day today repeat this verse: "For God so loved the world that he gave his only Son, that whoever believes in him should not perish but have eternal life" (Jn 3:16). What might you do today in response to God's extravagant love for you?

Contemplation: As you come to the end of this time of prayer, be attentive to what God has revealed to you today.

Week 1, Day 7:

Summary, Week 1

On the last day of each week you will be asked to spend your thirty-minute prayer time reflecting upon how God has been moving in your life during the previous week. Today you are invited to be aware of what has been revealed to you as you have explored the metaphor of God as "Father."

Reading: Spend some time reviewing your daily work-book experiences. Read with an openness to what you see revealed in those pages.

Meditation: The following questions may help to guide your reflections about your prayer experiences of this week:

1.   What were the most important things you discovered about God during this week?

2.   What did you learn about yourself as you explored this metaphor?

3.   Can you identify some of your feelings during this week (for example, comfort, challenge, love, etc.)?

Perhaps different days created different feelings for you. If
so, explain.

4. Is there anything you feel called to do as a result of
your reflections this week? If so, what will you need to do
to respond to this calling?

5.   What questions or concerns do you have that relate to your experience this week?

Response: Offer to God whatever prayers seem to respond to your experience of this week.

Contemplation: In silence, be aware of what has been revealed to you during your prayer time today.

WEEK TWO

Parental Metaphors:
God as Mother

Week 2, Day 1:

God Our Mother, "In Whom We Live and Move and Have Our Being"

This week you are invited to explore the metaphor of God as Mother. The biblical writers used masculine metaphors to talk about their experiences of God much more frequently than they used feminine ones. But they did not use *only* male images. A variety of metaphors point to experiences of God as one who has feminine qualities as well.

You may find it difficult, at first, to conceive of God in feminine terms. Most Christians have not been accustomed to talking about God using other than masculine words. The church, whose leadership has been predominantly male since its very beginnings, has often ignored references in the scriptures that characterize God as feminine. Most of the church's hymnals, worship books, and curriculum resources, until recent years, have used exclusively male language for God. There are only a few daring spiritual pilgrims over the centuries whose writings point to prayer lives rich in both masculine and feminine experiences of God.

These feminine metaphors are indeed a "rich treasury" for our prayer lives. Feminine words for God can help to expand our awareness of how God is involved in our lives. When we explore these metaphors in prayer, we are invited to observe God's activity in us and in our world in ways that we do not see when we use only the familiar, mostly masculine, words for God. We have become accustomed to thinking of God as Father. But what new, growth-inspiring awareness of God's activity will we see when we consider that God also relates to us as Mother? I invite you to be open now to what God may reveal to you as you as you explore the metaphor of God as Mother.

Reading: Begin your prayer time in silence. Then read
Acts 17:22–28. Remember as you read that devotional
reading is to be done with an openness to what God may
reveal to us. Reading aloud can facilitate our hearing of
God's word for us.

Meditation: In this sermon to the people of Athens, the
apostle Paul says that God is one in whom we, and people of every nation, "live and move and have our being"
(v 28). Here, and elsewhere in the Bible (see 2 Cor 5:17),
we are reminded that our true life is found "in God," or
"in Christ." Today I invite you to consider the human experience of one life "living" and "moving" and "having its
being" inside of another. The most common such experience is life in a mother's womb.
     Imagine what it would be like for you to return to
your mother's womb, where your life had its beginnings.
Of course, none of us can remember this existence from
our own experience of it. But we can imagine what such
an existence would be like. In the womb you are warm
and comfortable, secure in the surroundings that become
more and more familiar to you the longer you are there.
In the womb you also are protected from harm. Aware of
the constant rhythm of your mother's heartbeat, you rest
without fear. You are nurtured in the womb; your mother
supplies you with everything you need to grow.
     Life in your mother's womb is a very comfortable ex-
istence, but it is not a static one. In the womb you are constantly growing and exploring. Your body is being formed
in its own unique fashion. Eventually you begin to move
and kick and suck your thumb. You are so small, and yet
few moments pass when your mother is not aware of you.
She rejoices in the new life that is being formed within
her, delighting in the feel of your movements and in the
sound of your heartbeat. As the months continue, and
you become heavier and heavier, she bears the burden
of carrying you, awaiting the day of your birth. You are
not aware, as you safely rest in your mother's womb, how
very deeply she loves you!

1.   From this passage of scripture, and your reflections upon it, what did you learn about God? yourself? the world?

2.   Recall a time in your life when you felt protected or nurtured or comforted by God. How did it feel to receive God's presence in this way?

Response: In your verbal prayers, give thanks to God for God's presence in your life, and ask God to help you to be aware of your life "in" God today.

Throughout the day be aware that you "live and move and have your being" in God, your Mother. Be attentive to the difference it makes in the day's activities.

Contemplation: Return to silence, being open to what God has revealed to you during this time of prayer.

Week 2, Day 2:

God Our Mother, Giver of New Birth

Reading: Begin your prayer time in silence. Then read Romans 8:18–25.

Meditation: Yesterday you were invited to reflect upon the security of life in the womb. You also were asked to observe the love a mother has for the life within her as she anticipates the birth of her child. Today, as you meditate upon this scripture text, consider the process of giving birth.

Take note, first of all, of the words in this passage that describe the struggles of labor and childbirth: "eager longing" (v 19), "groaning in travail" (v 22, 23), "wait" (v 23), and "hope" (v 24).

1.   Write in this space words that describe what it is like to be in labor. Women who have given birth to children may draw upon their own experience. Others will need to rely upon the experiences of those who have known "labor pains." Spend a few moments reflecting upon this experience.

Reread verses 22–23. Paul pictures creation, and us, experiencing suffering and futility at the present time. He compares these sufferings with the travail of labor, as we long for the promised new creation to be revealed. But we are not alone in our struggle. God our Mother shares in the travail with us. God suffers alongside us as God's purposes are hindered by the evils of this world.

2.   Think about our world today. Where do you see the travail of suffering and futility?

In this passage we also find great words of promise. Reread verse 18. Many women who have given birth to children claim that there is no pain greater than the pain of childbirth. But when the child is born, and the parents behold the newborn baby, the anguish of labor soon is forgotten. As surely as God our Mother participates with us in the travail of the present time, God also promises us a glorious new birth. We receive the "first fruits" of that which is to be born through God's Spirit (v 23).

3.   When you consider the Christian church and the world, what "first fruits" or signs do you see that God is giving birth to the "new creation"?

Response: In your verbal prayers today, be aware of the sufferings of people in your own community and throughout the world. Remember to pray for yourself and for the church as God seeks to work through us to respond to suffering.

Consider something you might do to participate with God in the process of giving birth to the new creation. What can you do today to respond to the "travail" of others in the present time?

Contemplation: Return to silence, being aware of how God has been revealed to you as you end this time of prayer.

Week 2, Day 3:

Born of God Our Mother

Reading: Be still, knowing that God is with you as you begin this time of prayer. Read John 3:1–17.

Meditation: During yesterday's prayer time you were asked to consider a mother's experience of labor and childbirth. Today you are invited to reflect upon what the child experiences in the process of being born. While the womb conjures up images of warmth, comfort, and security, a child cannot remain in the womb forever. The nurture of the womb gives an important start to life, but if the fetus is to become a growing, healthy human person,

he or she must be given birth into the world. For a baby,
the process of being pushed from the womb, through the
birth canal, and into the strange, cold world is a traumatic
one. Being born is among the most shocking of the many
struggles in life that pave the way for human growth.

It can be comforting for us to picture ourselves ex-
isting peacefully within the womb of God, as we did two
days ago. But today I invite you to be aware that our life
with God also includes the challenge to accept new birth.

In our scripture text for today, Jesus spoke to Nicodemus about being "born anew." For each person such new
birth takes place in different ways. Jesus showed Nicodemus what being "pushed" into new life would entail for
him. Nicodemus, we are told, was a Pharisee, a ruler of
the Jews. For Nicodemus, being religious meant unques-
tioning adherence to a set of rules and regulations that
were "born of the flesh" (v 6). His was a religion based
upon rewards and admiration for being "obedient," and
punishment and degradation for "disobedience." Could
it be that Nicodemus came to Jesus that night because
he still was not satisfied with his life, in spite of all he
had done to attain his religious success? What Nicodemus needed, according to Jesus, was not to accomplish
something else, but to let go of his desire to succeed. If he
could learn that his true worth was found in God's love
for him, not in his many accomplishments, Nicodemus
would make a great step toward "new life."

It would have been painful, even traumatic, for Nicodemus to let go of his quest for rewards and admiration,
similar to the shock of being born. Imagine how difficult it
would be for this Pharisee to begin to identify with "out-
casts" and "sinners"! But also imagine the joy and contentment he would find in his new life with God!

1.   Nicodemus' encounter with Jesus challenged him
toward new life. Recall an important experience in your
life which pushed or nudged you toward the faith you
now hold.

2.   Where are you being called to grow at the present
time? What do you feel God is calling you to do in order
to enable this growth? How are you resisting this growth?

3.   For Nicodemus, to respond to Jesus' invitation would
have meant making sacrifices. But there would be joyous
benefits for him as well. What do you see as the sacrifices
and benefits for you if you were to respond to the invitation for "new life"?

Response: As you respond to God in a verbal prayer today, continue to be aware of the direction toward which
God may be moving you in receiving "new birth." Ask
God for the wisdom, courage, and strength to be "born
anew."

   During the day today call this verse to mind: "Beloved, let us love one another; for love is of God, and
[whoever] loves is born of God and knows God. [Who-
ever] does not love does not know God; for God is love"
(I Jn 4:7–8). Do something for someone today that would
be an expression of your love for them.

Contemplation: As you end your prayer time in silence, be
aware of God's presence with you.

Week 2, Day 4:

God Our Mother Nurtures Us

Reading: In silence, know that God's love surrounds
you as you begin your prayer time today. Read Isaiah
49:14–18.

Meditation: At the time this message from Isaiah first was proclaimed, the people of Israel were in distress. Their towns had been devastated by their enemies. Many of the people had died in battle; others had been carried off to live in bondage in a foreign land. With no home and no hope, they cried, "The Lord has forsaken me, my Lord has forgotten me" (v 14).

1.   What is it that makes you most concerned or afraid at the present time?

Now read verse 15. Isaiah assured God's troubled people that they were not forgotten. He compared God's care for them with the care of a nursing mother toward her child.

In an article entitled, "In the Circle of a Mother's Arms," Wendy M. Wright describes what she has learned about God and prayer through her experience as a nursing mother:

> A woman who is nursing must learn attentiveness to the particular moment.... Attentiveness tends to focus a mother on the presence of her child, to enable her to perceive his or her unique face, hands, and body in a contemplative way, to see her baby as the mysterious gift of person that he or she truly is.[1]

God our Mother is attentive to our needs like a nursing mother is attentive to the needs of her child.

2. Pause for a moment now and focus upon God's attentiveness to you. How does this awareness help you with the concern or fear you expressed in question #1? Make some notes in this space.

Wright continues to describe her experience as a nursing mother:

> A related spiritual art learned in nursing is the art of giving of one's own substance. Human milk is a substance obtained only at the cost of giving of one's own life energy. The nutrients stored in a woman's cells, the energy derived from the food she eats and the liquids she drinks, all are channeled into the production of milk. . . . Nursing draws upon one's deepest, most essential body resources.[2]

Our meditations on God as nursing mother remind us, too, of God's self-giving love in response to our needs. God showed us the depth of that love in Jesus Christ, who suffered death upon a cross, the ultimate act of self-giving, for our salvation.

3. In what ways might you order your daily activities to receive the nurture of God's presence?

Response: As you express your prayers to God, recall times when God has nurtured you and give thanks for them. Ask God to help you to be attentive to God and to those around you today.

Think about some particular thing you will do several times during the day today (for example, eating, making phone calls, etc.). Take a moment each time you are about to do this activity to remember that God is attentive to you and desires to nurture you throughout the day.

Contemplation: In silence, spend some time being attentive to how God has been revealed to you during your prayer time today.

Week 2, Day 5:

God Our Mother Invites Us Into Family

Reading: Be still in the presence of God. Then read Luke 13:31–34.

Meditation: We live in a world that is badly in need of a vision of community. Fear, distrust, and competitiveness often result in isolation between individuals and within societies and churches. As individuals pursue their own interests without regard for others, they create stress and broken relationships. Struggles between groups in a society to assert their power over others can lead to violence, discrimination, and a widening gap between those who have much and those who have little. Even within the church, we may perceive ourselves as scattered individuals who gather occasionally for worship, rather than as a community of the faithful whose life together is marked by support and care for one another.

1. Can you give any specific examples that show the present need for community? Write one or two of them here. What do you see as the consequences of the lack of community?

2. What do you see in your own life that may hinder your experience of community with others?

From time to time courageous individuals come to offer us a vision of community. They confront the competitiveness that makes us look at each other as "enemies." They challenge our prejudices, calling us to relate to all people with love and justice. They invite us to reorder our consumptive lifestyles so that all members of the human family can be fed, clothed, and housed. Hearing their call, we often ignore it. Many of these prophetic ones have been imprisoned and martyred for confronting the forces that hinder community. While their vision offers hope for all people, it is a great threat to the powerful who are satisfied with the way things are.

Jesus offered a vision of community to the people of his day, and they nailed him to a cross! In this text, as Herod schemed to kill him, Jesus cried in anguish over the people of God who would not receive God's messengers. Using a metaphor that is found frequently in the Psalms (see Ps 17:8–9; 61:4; 91:4), he declared, "How often would I have gathered your children together as a hen gathers her brood under her wings, and you would not!" (v 34b).

3.   Take some time now to reflect upon this image of a hen gathering together her family. What words best describe for you what life would be like for a chick who is sheltered under its mother's wings?

4. What do you learn about God, and your relationship with God, as you think about the metaphor of a mother hen?

5. What is implied in this metaphor about community? (Think about the relationships between the hen and her chicks and the relationships among the chicks within the brood.)

Response: Give thanks for what God has revealed to you today.

Repent of specific ways in which you may have hindered community.

Pray for peace in your own life, in your family, in the
church, and throughout the world.

During the day today consider what could be done to
enhance the sense of community in your church and in the
world. Make some notes below. What does God want you
to do to assist in building community?

Contemplation: Return to silence, being open to God's
presence with you as a member of God's family.

Week 2, Day 6:

God Our Mother Empowers Us

Reading: Reading that is most beneficial to our prayer
lives is done slowly and carefully. Relax for a few moments in the silence of this place, then read this verse
several times:

> Like an eagle teaching its
>   young to fly,
>   catching them safely on its
>   spreading wings,

the Lord kept Israel from
   falling.
— Deuteronomy 32:11 (Good News Bible)

Meditation: During this week you have been invited to
explore the metaphor of God as Mother. You have been
asked to consider various aspects of the mother-child relationship, from the existence within the womb, through
the processes of labor and childbirth, to the experiences of
being nurtured and made part of a family. Today I invite
you to meditate upon a primary goal of a mother's presence in our lives: to empower us.

Picture the mother eagle teaching one of its eaglets to
fly. She nudges it out of the security of the nest into the
spacious sky. At first the baby eagle flounders, flaps its
wings frantically, but soon plunges toward the ground.
The mother eagle never loses sight of her young. Before
the eaglet is harmed, its mother swoops down, spreads
her wings, and catches it. Almost in an instant she returns
her young to the nest, only to nudge it out again, and
again, and again. There are many feeble attempts made by
this eaglet at flying. It seems cruel for its mother to continue dropping it from the nest. But, in time, the young
eagle learns to fly. Its wings become stronger and stronger
until it soars with power and speed high into the sky.
We gaze with a sense of awe and wonder at the eagle in
flight. Yet, without the nudge of its mother out of the nest,
it would not learn to fly.

1.   Recall a time in your life when you floundered or fell.
As you think back over that situation, how do you feel
God was present in it?

2.   What do you consider to be your greatest strength as a
Christian?

3.   In what area(s) of your life do you feel you most need
to be empowered by God?

Response: In your verbal prayers today, remember to
thank God for God's presence in your life during difficult
times. Ask God to strengthen you in the areas of weak-
ness you have identified. Pray for the grace to use your
strength to glorify God today.

    During the day, reflect upon these words to the chil-
dren of Israel, "You have seen what I did to the Egyptians,
and how I bore you on eagle's wings and brought you to
myself." Make these words your own today.

Contemplation: End your prayer time as it began: in silence. Be attentive to what God has revealed to you in
prayer today.

Week 2, Day 7:

Summary, Week 2

Today you are asked to spend your thirty-minute prayer time reflecting upon how God has been moving in your life this week as you have explored the metaphor of God as Mother.

Reading: Review your daily workbook experiences. Read with an openness to what you see revealed in those pages.

Meditation: The following questions may help to guide your reflections about your prayer experiences of this week:

1.   What were the most important things you discovered about God during this week?

2.   What did you learn about yourself as you explored
this metaphor?

3.   Can you identify some of your feelings during this
week (for example, comfort, challenge, love, etc.)? Perhaps different days created different feelings for you. If so,
explain.

4. Is there anything you feel called to do as a result of your reflections this week? If so, what will you need to do to respond to this calling?

5. What questions or concerns do you have that relate to your experience of this week?

Response: Offer to God whatever prayers seem to respond to your experience this week.

Contemplation: In silence, be aware of what has been revealed to you during your prayer time today.

Notes

1 Wendy M. Wright, "In the Circle of a Mother's Arms," in *Weavings* 1 (January/February, 1988), p. 17.

2 Ibid., p. 18.

WEEK THREE

Occupational Metaphors:
Part I

Week 3, Day 1:

God the Midwife

Biblical writers often drew upon the experiences of everyday life to describe how God was being revealed to God's people. At the center of daily life for both women and men were their various occupations. In this section you are invited to explore metaphors for God that relate God's presence to tasks that were commonplace in the lives of biblical people. Hopefully, as you use these metaphors in prayer, you will discover more fully how God is present in your life.

Reading: When you have relaxed in your place of silence, read Isaiah 66:7–11.

Meditation: Last week you were asked to focus upon the experiences of mother and child as they relate to God's presence in your life and in the world. Today I invite you to explore another person who played an important part in the birthing process: the midwife. The profession of midwife was valued highly in biblical times (see Exodus 1, for example). To be a midwife one needed a variety of qualities. A midwife had to have skill and experience in order to instruct the mother during the process of giving birth. She needed to be physically strong to facilitate the movement of the child as it was being delivered. To be a midwife also required gentleness. She had to be able to reassure and encourage a woman who was writhing in the pain of labor. She had to be clean and meticulous as she cleaned the baby and the mother and placed the child at its mother's breast. When we consider the responsibilities involved in this occupation, it is no wonder that midwives were so highly regarded in Israel.

The writer of this section of Isaiah looks out over the land of Israel as God's people are returning from exile in a foreign land. He sees them struggling to restore this land which has been devastated by its oppressor. And he proclaims that God will relate to them as a midwife relates to a mother during childbirth. Having been released from the land of exile, they were free. Yet there was still much rebuilding to be done before they could be the people God intended them to be. The prophet came to bring good news to God's struggling people. They would not be alone in the process of restoration. God the Midwife would be present to care for them, and to give them strength and encouragement!

In Jesus Christ God offers us freedom from the bondage of sin and death. Yet, when we look at our lives, we realize that there is still much restoration to be done. We have not yet fully experienced the promised fruits of "love, joy, peace, patience, kindness, goodness, faithfulness, gentleness, and self-control" (Gal 5:22–23) in our own lives or in our churches. But, like God's people long ago, we have this assurance that God the Midwife is present through the Holy Spirit to strengthen and encourage, enabling these fruits to be born in us.

1. As you reflect upon the metaphor of God as Midwife, what new insights come to you about God and God's involvement in your life and in the world?

2. In what area do you feel you most need strength and encouragement in your life at the present time?

3. Where do you see the need for continuing "restoration" in your church? In what areas of your church do you feel the most strengthening and encouragement are needed? What can you do to enable restoration in those areas?

Response: In your verbal prayers today, give thanks for times in your life when you were given strength and encouragement, and for the people through whom you received it. Ask God to help you to be open to the work of restoration God desires to do in you. Pray for your church, especially in those areas where it has particular needs.

During the day today try to think of some specific thing you can do to facilitate the growth of your church. Share the idea with your pastor or with another member of your church.

Contemplation: Be still as your prayer time ends for today, remembering that God is with you.

Week 3, Day 2:

God the Potter

Reading: After your time of silence, as you are becoming focused upon God's presence, read Jeremiah 18:1–11.

Meditation: "Behold, like the clay in the potter's hand, so are you in my hand, O house of Israel" (v 6b). Like Jeremiah, Adelaide A. Pollard uses the metaphor of God as Potter to describe God's presence in our lives in the hymn "Have Thine Own Way." Spend a few moments now allowing these words to touch your life.

> Have thine own way, Lord! Have thine own
>   way!
> Thou art the potter; I am the clay.
> Mold me and make me After thy will,
> While I am waiting, Yielded and still.

Consider, first of all, the relationship between the potter and the clay. The potter creates by giving form to the formless. In the potter's hand, the clay is pliable, able to

be molded and shaped. Notice that it is God the Potter
who does the shaping. Whether we choose to be or not,
we are like the clay, to be molded in the Potter's hand.

1. Sometimes we only see the shaping work of God in us
after it has taken place. Recall a particular time in your life
when God was working to help you to become the person
you are now, although you may not have been aware of it
at the time.

2. What can you learn from that experience about what
God may be doing in your life in the present?

While God's work often gives shape to our lives without us being aware of it, our openness to God can facilitate God's work. The hymn uses the words "waiting," "yielded," and "still" to describe our attentiveness to the Potter.

3. Spend at least five minutes now being completely still. With both of your feet on the floor and your hands comfortably on your lap, close your eyes and try not to move. In the stillness, focus on your breathing. Feel the air as it moves in and out of your nostrils. Simply yield to God's presence.

Sometimes stillness is comforting to us; it can be a respite during a day of much activity. At other times it is a challenge to us. We may feel that it's a waste of time when there are so many things to be done. Jeremiah talks about the pottery being "plucked up, broken down, and destroyed" so that a new vessel can be created. Perhaps one of the things that needs to be reworked in us is our need to be constantly doing something. We need to learn to be still, emptying ourselves of the many things that distract us, so that we can be yielded as clay in the Potter's hand.

4. Spend another five minutes in stillness. This time be aware of what enters your mind as you try to be still.

Our "wanderings of mind" can tell us much about ourselves, and about what concerns us most at the present
time. It can be helpful for us to be attentive to them. Following your time of stillness, make some notes below
about your thoughts. What may God be revealing to you
during this time?

Response: For your verbal prayers today, read aloud the
words of the hymn, "Have Thine Own Way." Speak to
God whatever you feel led to pray as a result of your
meditations.

During the day, set apart at least two five-minute
time periods to return to the stillness, as instructed in #3
above. You may wish to continue the practice of stillness
every day, pausing several times to be aware of God's
presence with you. Each time you become still, be attentive to what God is revealing to you about your need for
"waiting" and "yielding."

Contemplation: In silence, focus upon what God has revealed to you during your prayer time today.

Week 3, Day 3:

God the Shepherd Cares for Us

Reading: In silence yield to God, who desires to care for you. Then read Psalm 23. Remember to read for formation. Perhaps you will wish to read this psalm aloud slowly, several times.

Meditation: The metaphor of God as Shepherd is one of the most familiar and comforting in all of scripture. Turn your attention toward this figure now, seeing what new insights into God and yourself you may receive today.

1. One thing I notice as I read this psalm is that God the Shepherd not only directs the sheep, but also is open to their needs. How a shepherd leads is influenced by the situation of the sheep. Take several minutes now to write down all the phrases you can find in this psalm that describe the activity of a shepherd. (For example, in verse 2 the Psalmist sings that the Shepherd "makes me lie down in green pastures.")

2. Now that you have made note of the Psalmist's experience of the shepherd, consider your own experience. Take some time to put this psalm into your own words,

mindful of your own experience of God. (For example, the first part of verse 2 could be rewritten to say: "Once I was anxious about a certain problem and I could not get to sleep. I prayed to the Lord, my Shepherd, and I was comforted and was able to rest.")

Response: In your prayers today, give praise for the ways God has "shepherded" you. Pray for openness to how God may wish to be present in your life today as you go about your daily activities.

During the day today, recall the promise of this verse several times: "I know that your goodness and love will be with me all my life; and your house will be my home as long as I live" (v 6 Good News Bible).

Contemplation: Be still and consider for a moment what has been revealed to you during this time of prayer.

Week 3, Day 4:

God the Shepherd Seeks the Lost

Reading: After your silent time, read Luke 15:1–7.

Meditation: Yesterday our focus was upon the Shepherd's care for us. Today I invite you to consider another aspect of the metaphor of God as Shepherd. In reading Psalm 23 we get a picture of a shepherd as a gentle person, tenderly caring for the sheep. But in Luke 15 we are reminded that shepherds also had to be rugged men and women. (Yes, women also cared for sheep in biblical times. See, for example, the story of Jacob and Rachel in Genesis 29:4–12.) Great risks often were taken by the shepherd in safeguarding the sheep. Shepherds spent long, rugged days in the wilderness, enduring the extremes of weather and the threats of wild animals. And, as we find in this passage, if a sheep were to become lost, the faithful shepherd would risk life and limb to find it.

As we meditate upon the metaphor of God as Shepherd, it can be helpful to identify with the characters in this story. First of all, consider the one sheep that was lost.

1. Who are the "lost" of today? How did they get lost?

2. In what ways can you identify with the "lost"? What is lost in you?

     Now observe the other sheep, the ninety-nine who were left by the shepherd in the search for the one that was lost.

3. What people or groups would you identify as the ninety-nine in our day? What does it mean to them that the shepherd left them "in the wilderness" to go searching for the one that was lost?

4. In what ways do you identify with the ninety-nine?

     Finally, consider the shepherd who took the risk of leaving the rest of the flock behind to search for the one who was lost.

5. What do you learn about God the Shepherd in this text?

6. In what ways do you identify with the Shepherd? How are you called to respond to the lost, and to the remainder of the flock?

Response: As you offer your verbal prayers today, be aware that God desires to hear your prayers. Invite God to redeem what is "lost" in you. Ask God to empower you as you participate in the Shepherd's ministry to the lost.

During the day today, consider your answer to question #6 above. What might you do today to respond to the call of God to seek and to save the lost?

Contemplation: Relax as your prayer time ends, being open to God's presence in your life.

Week 3, Day 5:

God the Homemaker

Reading: Be still for a few moments, appreciating the silence of your place of prayer. Then read Luke 15:8–10.

Meditation: You have been involved now for nearly three weeks in setting apart thirty minutes a day for prayer. Today, as you meditate on the metaphor of God as Homemaker, I invite you to consider what is happening to you as a result of your prayers.

Observe the three acts of the woman who is cleaning her house in search of the lost coin. She "lights a lamp," "sweeps the floor," and "seeks diligently" until she finds it. We may view God's activity in us through prayer using these words.

In prayer there is a certain enlightening that takes place. As we are open to God's presence in us, we receive new insights into our relationships with God and others. We also discover some things about ourselves.

1.   Recall some of the most important things that have been revealed to you in your journey of prayer during the past few weeks. Make some notes.

Sometimes the enlightenment that comes to us in prayer is comforting to us. At other times it is disconcerting. We may have become comfortable in the darkness of some habit, or prejudice, or manner of relating to others. When the light is turned on, what is unclean is revealed. God the Homemaker desires to cleanse us from those things that hinder our relationship with God and with others. God also desires a cleansing from the hindrances to our own growth as persons made in God's image.

2.   What uncleanness is being exposed in you? What is it that God desires to sweep clean in your life?

Not only does the light reveal what needs to be cleaned. It also reveals what is lost. Sometimes homemakers are involved in cleaning. At other times they are involved in searching for lost things.

3.   Have you discovered anything during these weeks that God is still seeking out in you? Is there some part of your life that you have not yet committed totally to God?

Response: Give thanks for God's work in you as you have set apart time for prayer.

Confess your need to grow in your love for God and others. Ask God to give you the grace you need to be open to God's continuing work in you.

During the day today, reflect upon the importance of setting apart a time for prayer.

Contemplation: Be still, yielding yourself to God, as you end your prayer time in silence.

Week 3, Day 6:

God the Employer

Reading: When you have become still, read Matthew 20:1–16.

Meditation: As you begin to consider God as Employer, focus on the first part of this parable, verses 1–7. Here we find laborers being sent out into the vineyard. As the householder was determined that no one would be standing idle when there was work to be done in the vineyard, so God seeks to employ us in labors for the kingdom.

1.   Describe the vineyard in which you feel God is calling you to serve.

2. What are the greatest needs in that place at the present time? What do you feel God wants you to do to respond to those needs?

Now spend some time with the second part of this parable, verses 8–16. Observe how the householder pays the laborers. Those who worked only one hour received the same wage as those who labored the entire day. At first it seems so unfair that those who serve in God's vineyard their whole lives receive the same reward as those who serve only during the "eleventh hour" of their lives. Yet, when we think about the benefits received by those who labor long in God's vineyard, we realize that our Employer's generosity is great indeed!

3.   What are the benefits you have received from your labors in the vineyard? What are the challenges and struggles for God's laborers?

Response: In your verbal prayers today, be aware of the needs of the vineyard in which you are called to serve. Ask God to help you in your labors. Give thanks for the benefits you receive from your life in the Householder's vineyard.

During the day, return to question #2 above. Do something today to respond to a need you have identified in God's vineyard.

Contemplation: Close your prayer time as you usually do, in silent attentiveness to God.

Week 3, Day 7:

Summary, Week 3

As you come to the end of another week, you are invited to spend your thirty-minute prayer time pulling together some of your reflections about God's movement in your life as you have explored occupational metaphors for God.

Reading: Review your daily workbook experiences. Read with an openness to what you see revealed in those pages.

Meditation: The following questions may help to guide your reflections about your prayer experiences of this week.

1.   What are the most important things you discovered about God during this week?

2.   What did you learn about yourself as you explored these metaphors?

3.   Can you identify some of your feelings during this week (for example, comfort, challenge, love, etc.)? Perhaps different days created different feelings for you. If so, explain.

4.   Is there anything you feel called to do as a result of your reflections this week? If so, what will you need to do to respond to this calling?

5.   What questions or concerns do you have that relate to your experience this week?

Response: Offer to God whatever prayers seem to respond to your experience of this week.

Contemplation: In silence, be aware of what has been revealed to you during your prayer time today.

WEEK FOUR

Occupational Metaphors:
Part II

Week 4, Day 1:

God the Sower

Reading: Spend a few moments now in silence, being attentive to God's presence with you. Then read Matthew 13:1–9, 18–23.

Meditation: In the introduction to this book I explained that one of its purposes is to invite you to experience a style of prayer called *lectio divina*. You may wish to continue using *lectio divina* on your own after you have completed this six-week study. One way of doing that is to choose a certain theme, such as a particular metaphor for God, and to use various passages of scripture related to that theme in your daily prayer time. This has been our approach so far. Another way of using *lectio divina* is to work through an entire section or book of the Bible. During this week you will be asked to use *lectio divina* to explore Matthew 13. We find, as we look at the parables of the kingdom, that they are fraught with occupational metaphors for God.

As you meditate upon this familiar parable of the sower, I invite you to be aware that God is always being revealed to you. The Sower is ever scattering seeds and desiring for us to be receptive to them. Some are seeds of wisdom, helping us to see the truth about ourselves and the world around us. Others are seeds of hope, giving us comfort and strength during difficult times. Still others are seeds of love, reminding us that we have worth in God's eyes and challenging us to relate in loving ways toward others.

1.   What other seeds do you see being cast about by the Sower in your life and in the world around you?

In this parable we see not only how the sower scatters seeds, but also how well the ground is prepared. The seeds are spread about, but the ground is not always very open to them. It would probably be more comforting for you to identify others who are unreceptive or shallow when it comes to their openness to God. But we miss the intent of this parable if we neglect to observe how it relates to our own lives. Consider how receptive you are to the seeds God the Sower desires to plant in you. What hinders you from being more open to God?

2.   Reread verses 3–7 and 19–22 of this parable. Where do you see yourself as you consider the hindrances of "misunderstanding," "shallowness," and "world-weariness"? Which of these most hinders your openness to God's seeds?

3. What can you do to be more open to God?

4. Now reread verses 8–9 and 23. How have you been
receptive to God's seeds? What has resulted from your
openness?

Response: In your verbal prayers today, be thankfully
aware of the seeds God has scattered in your life, even
those that have challenged you most. Repent of the things
that hinder your openness to God, and ask for the grace to
be more receptive to God.

During the day today look for "seeds" God is sowing
in you and in the world. As you observe any, make note
of them.

Contemplation: As you come to the end of this prayer
time, silently be attentive to the seeds God has sown in
you during this time.

Week 4, Day 2:

God the Householder

Reading: Following your period of silence, read Matthew 13:24–30, 36–43.

Meditation: Observe the servants in this parable. They saw that the evil one had sown weeds among the wheat, so they went to the householder and said, "Do you want us to go and gather them?" Notice how the householder responded: "No; lest in gathering the weeds you root up the wheat along with them." The servants were not to try to separate the wheat from the tares. They were called to care for the entire field until the time of the harvest. It is the householder, not the servants, who is responsible for separating the good from the evil.

Focus now on what this parable has to say to us about our relationships with others. Often we, the servants of God, try to do what it is not in our place to do. We try to separate the "wheat," from the "weeds." The wheat are those who are deemed by us to be worthy of life in the kingdom. They are of value in our eyes because they are good or moral or religious or "like us." The weeds are the unworthy ones. They are to be criticized because we see them as bad or immoral or pagan or "not our kind."

1.   Who do you see as "weeds" in our society today?

2. Can you name any specific individuals or groups of people with whom you find it most difficult to relate (for example, minorities, homosexuals, unpleasant neighbors, etc.)?

We run into trouble, you see, when we try to separate the wheat from the tares. In our attempts to do the harvesting of the wheat and the plucking out of the weeds, we may get some weeds mixed in with the wheat or we may throw some of the wheat into the fire. It is not possible for us to judge how another person really stands in relationship to God. We are called to care for everyone, regardless of how unworthy they may seem in our eyes.

Jesus declared, "You shall love your neighbor as yourself." In his life and teaching he showed us that such love does not have conditions attached to it. He loved everyone, including those whom his society called unworthy, or "outsiders." Servants of God are commanded to relate to others in this same way.

3. In light of your answer to question #2 above, what would it mean for you to relate in loving ways to *everyone*?

4.   What could you do today to care both for those.
whom society calls "wheat" and those whom it calls
"weeds"? What difference would that make in your life
and in the lives of others?

Response: In your prayers today, ask God to forgive you
for the conditions you place on your love for others. Pray
for the courage and strength to love everyone in God's
field.

During the day today call this verse to mind several
times: "From now on, therefore, we regard no one from
a human point of view; even though we once regarded
Christ from a human point of view, we regard him thus
no longer. Therefore if anyone is in Christ he [or she] is a
new creation; the old has passed away, behold, the new
has come" (2 Cor 5:16–17).

Contemplation: As you come to the end of your prayer time today, be open to what God has revealed to you.

Week 4, Day 3:

God the Planter, Who Sees Great Possibilities

Reading: When in silence you have become attentive to God, read Matthew 13:31–32.

Meditation: So far this week we have focused on metaphors for God that would have been meaningful to the men and women who did the work of planting and harvesting in Jesus' time. Our meditations during the first two days have been related to the meaning of these farming metaphors for our lives as individuals as we relate to God (receiving God's "seeds") and as we relate to others (caring for "wheat" and "weeds"). As we come to the third agricultural metaphor for God, I invite you to consider the mission of your church.

Fix in your mind, first of all, the picture Jesus draws in this parable. A planter takes a mustard seed, "the smallest of all seeds" (v 32), and carefully sows it in the ground. Each day the planter returns to the place where the seed was planted to observe the plant's growth and to nurture it. At first, it appears that nothing will become of that tiny seed. But, although there is no evidence of growth above the ground, already the seed is beginning to open and sprout beneath the soil. Gradually, as the rains come and the sun shines, the tiny plant pushes through the soil. Dry periods hinder the plant's growth. Predators threaten to destroy it. But with the gentle care of the gardener, the mustard plant grows to become "the greatest of shrubs and becomes a tree, so that the birds of the air come and make nests in its branches" (v 32).

Now, think about what this parable implies about the mission of the church in the world. Consider that the church is like that tiny mustard seed which God the Planter sows and cares for.

1. When you look at your church in its community, in what ways, if any, does it appear to be the "smallest of all seeds," whose growth often goes unnoticed?

2. Would you say that your church at the present time is in a dry period, or in a period where the gentle rains and warm sunshine are causing growth? What evidence can you give of this?

3. What "predators" threaten your church at the present time?

4. As you read this parable, what do you learn about the future of the Christian church? How is God to be involved in making future possibilities become realities?

5. Think about one specific way your church could enable growth to take place. (Remember, "growth" does not mean just numerical growth. This may be included, but there are other ways churches can grow.) What is God calling you to do to participate in your church's growth?

Response: Give thanks to God for your church today. Remember to pray for its ministry both within its fellowship and in the community and the world beyond its walls.

During the day today share your meditations on question #5 with someone in your church, and with your pastor. Let these words be upon your lips throughout the day today: "So we are ambassadors for Christ, God making [God's] appeal through us. We beseech you on behalf of Christ, be reconciled to God" (2 Cor 5:20).

Contemplation: As you close this time of prayer, listen to what God would reveal to you.

Week 4, Day 4:

God the Bakerwoman

Reading: We have seen before how, when we read for "formation," a single verse of scripture can engage us for a long period of time. It would be possible to read this verse in a matter of seconds, if we were reading for "information." But if it is to make its claim upon our lives, we need to "chew on it" for a time. Read Matthew 13:33 aloud several times, slowly.

Meditation: At this point in our journey it is important to note that Jesus was careful to include occupations performed by women as well as those performed by men when he talked about life in the realm of God. In the Hebrew culture, for example, both women and men were involved in the work of farming. Scattering seed, planting, nurturing, and gathering the harvest were tasks in which every member of the family took part. God, who is neither male nor female, is revealed to us in the experiences of both men and women. This is seen quite clearly in Jesus' parable of the woman baking bread.

Perhaps you have memories of entering a kitchen where someone was baking bread. I remember how, as a child, I would often be found in my grandmother's kitchen where the aroma of bread baking would make my mouth water. I could hardly wait to get a taste of it.

It is an amazing process — a few measures of flour being transformed into a loaf of bread. The proper. amount of every ingredient is essential. One of the most important ingredients, of course, is the leaven. Leaven is dynamic. When it is "hid" in flour it penetrates and changes that flour until it is completely different than it was at the start. Leaven is indeed a "change agent" in the process of baking bread.

Change is always taking place in our world and in our lives. Sometimes it takes place rapidly, almost in an instant. At other times it happens gradually, over a long period of time. Some change is good. It brings progress and enhances life within the local and global communities into which God calls us. But other change is evil. It inhibits human potential, and causes discord and hurt. Jesus Christ, whom John's gospel called "the bread of life" (Jn 6), came to bring positive transformation into the relationships of people with God and with one another. He also called his followers to be agents of change as they proclaimed the gospel in the world around them.

1.   Like hidden leaven, the effects of change often are seen only after the change has already taken place. As you think over your life, consider a major change that has taken place in you as a result of being a Christian. Make some notes about it in the space below.

2. Can you give some examples of changes for the better that have taken place in recent times? What are some
changes for evil that have taken place? How do you see
God involved in these changes?

3. As noted above, Christ calls us to be agents of change.
Identify a particular area in the church or in your community where you see a need for change. What might you do
to make such change a possibility?

Response: In your verbal prayers, be open to areas in your own life in which God may be desiring to bring change. Ask for the grace you need to allow the transforming work of Christ to take place in you. Also, pray for your church and the world, being especially aware of areas in which you see the need for change.

During the day today do something that will help to bring about change for the cause of Christ. Make some notes here about your experience.

Contemplation: Close with silence, being attentive to what God has revealed to you during this time.

Week 4, Day 5:

God the Investor

Reading: When you have had a few moments of silence, read Matthew 13:44–46.

Meditation: You are probably becoming aware that there are many ways to approach a single passage of scripture. In your reflections on the Bible readings, you may have found that God took you in a totally different direction than the meditative guides suggested. If that has happened to you, great! A primary goal of prayer is for you to be open to what God chooses to reveal to you personally. I invite you today to explore the metaphor of God as Investor using these two short parables. You will notice that a different approach will be suggested for your meditations on each one.

As you read the first parable again, remember how valuable you are to God. The cover story in a recent issue of *Time* magazine, entitled "The Rat Race: How America Is Running Out of Time," pointed out that people in our society today have become so busy with doing many things that they do not have time even for simple pleasures such as a relaxing meal with family or friends, reading a meaty novel, or observing a Sabbath day. Why this constant busyness? The author of the article contends that people need to be doing so many things in order to prove their worth to themselves and others.[1]

As we look at the world around us, we find that there is much truth to the *Time* writer's contention. People in our society are constantly trying to prove their value to others. They compete with one another, struggling to climb in their careers. They spend long hours hard at work, trying to accumulate much wealth. They make all sorts of sacrifices to prove that they are competent, productive, and worthwhile people. But notice, too, the consequences of this societal quest for value. We often neglect people who are seen as having little worth: the poor, minorities, the elderly, children, and the handicapped. They do not measure up to our image of success. Because we fear we will become like them and appear unworthy to others, we choose to avoid them.

But hear one of the refreshing promises of this parable: We have worth not because of our outward circumstances, but because God loves us. Every one of us, indeed the whole creation, is treasured by God. God, who loves us, willingly invests everything to possess us. The scriptures remind us over and over again of what a valuable investment we are to God the Investor. Look at John 3:16, for example.

1. As you think about the way you order your life at the present time, what do you do to try to prove that you are of worth?

2. How does it make you feel when you consider how valuable you are to God? What difference would it make in the way you order your life if you truly experienced your worth in God's sight?

Now that we have explored God's investment in us, consider your most valuable investments in life. Reread verses 45–46. Notice that when the merchant found that one pearl of priceless worth, he went and sold everything he had to buy it. In the same way, those who are in Christ are challenged to invest all they have in this most precious pearl: the kingdom.

3.   As you meditate on this parable, consider your priorities in life. To what things do you give primary loyalty? (Not what you desire to give primary loyalty to, but what you actually invest yourself in at the present time.) List them below, beginning with your highest priority.

4.   How do you feel about your present priorities in life?

5.   What would it mean for you to invest "all that you have" in the kingdom of God? What would be the sacrifices and the rewards for you if you would do this?

Response: As you express your prayers today, be aware of how precious you are to God. Confess areas in your life that you have not invested as yet in God. Ask God to give you the strength to put God first in your life.

During the day today, remember this verse, "But seek first God's kingdom and God's righteousness, and all these things will be yours as well." As you recall this verse, consider what God may be asking you to do to invest yourself more wholly in the kingdom.

Contemplation: Return now to silence, observing what God has revealed to you during this time today.

Week 4, Day 6:

God the Fisher

Reading: Be still and silent for a few moments. Then read Matthew 13:47–50.

Meditation: There is a certain uncompromising quality about life under the reign of God. The parables in Matthew 13 remind us, first of all, that God makes no compromise in relation to us. The Planter continues to nurture until the smallest seed becomes the greatest bush. The Baker hides leaven, and it doesn't stop working until all of the flour has been transformed by it. The Investor sells everything for the valued treasure and the precious pearl. God is indeed extravagant in dealing with us.

But these parables also remind us that no compromise is to be made by those who would live under the sovereignty of God. The seeds of the Sower are to be received and bring forth grain. While the wheat is to be gathered into the Householder's barn, the evil weeds are to be consumed by fire. We are called to invest all that we have in possessing the treasure that is life with God. While there is joy in these parables when we consider God's love for us, there is also challenge when we see what is entailed in our response to God's love. When we look at these parables, it seems that it is either all or nothing!

Observe the lack of compromise in the relation of the fisher to the fish in this parable. It is seen, first of all, in the net that is open to receive fish of every kind. God the Fisher is receptive to everyone. People of every kind, without discrimination, are welcome into life lived under the reign of God. And yet, while the fisher freely receives fish of every kind, we again find no compromise when the nets are hauled in and the fish are sorted out. The good fish, we are told, are put into vessels. But the bad are thrown away. In the same way, God the Fisher will not

compromise at the end of the age in separating the good
from the bad.

We are not told in this parable what makes a "good"
fish and what makes a "bad" one. It is the fisher and not
the fish who will ultimately decide that. But we do find
in the explanation of this parable a word used to describe
the good: "righteous" (v 49). Throughout the Bible, the
word "righteous" is used to describe right relationships
between God and humanity, and relationships with people to each other.[2] To be righteous means to be in loving
relationship with God. It is to love God "with all your
heart, and with all your soul, and with all your mind, and
with all your strength" (Mk 12:30). To be righteous also
means to respond to God's love by relating in loving ways
toward others. It is to "love your neighbor as yourself"
(Mk 12:31). We are moving in the direction of "righteousness," or of being "good" fish, when we are growing in
our love for God and for others. And such love is without
compromise.

1.   Spend a few moments reviewing your prayer times of
this week. What do you learn from your meditations on
these parables about the call to love God? How well are
you doing?

2. What do you learn in your review of these parables
about the call to love others? In what ways would you
like to improve?

3.   What do you feel you need to do to become more righteous?

Response: In your verbal prayers today, ask God to help you to become more loving in the way you relate to God and to others.

During the day be aware of your answer to question #3 above. Observe how your awareness of this goal to be righteous affects your life today.

Contemplation: Being in a state of silent yielding, receive whatever God would reveal to you as you come to the end of this time of prayer.

Week 4, Day 7:

Summary, Week 4

As you come to the end of this week, you are invited to spend your thirty-minute prayer time reviewing your reflections about God's movement in your life as you have explored the occupational metaphors for God.

Reading: Review your daily workbook experiences. Read with an openness to what you see revealed there.

Meditation: The following questions may help to guide your reflections about your prayer experiences this week:

1. What are the most important things you discovered about God during this week?

2. What did you learn about yourself as you explored these metaphors?

3.   Can you identify some of your feelings during this week (for example, comfort, challenge, love, etc.)? Perhaps different days created different feelings for you. If so, explain.

4.   Is there anything you feel called to do as a result of your reflections this week? If so, what will you need to do to respond to this calling?

5.   What questions or concerns do you have that relate to your experience of this week?

Response: Offer to God whatever prayers seem to respond to your experience of this week.

Contemplation: In silence, be aware of what has been revealed to you during your prayer time today.

Notes

1 Nancy Gibbs, "The Rat Race: How America Is Running Out of Time," *Time* 133 (April 24, 1989), p. 58.

2 Paul J. Achtemeier, "Righteousness in the New Testament," *The Interpreter's Dictionary of the Bible* (Nashville: Abingdon Press, 1962), p. 92.

WEEK FIVE

Metaphors of
Word and Wisdom

Week 5, Day 1:

God the Word Creates

In your times of prayer, you have been asked to explore both feminine and masculine metaphors for God. As you begin this final section, you are invited to look more closely at the meanings of the words *feminine* and *masculine*. The most common way of understanding these words is to associate them with the outer roles that women and men typically fulfill. As they articulated their experiences of God, biblical writers often used words that their hearers would commonly associate with the roles of women and men. In the first four weeks of this journey, feminine and masculine have been used in this way.

But feminine and masculine can also refer to "principles" or essential elements within both women and men. For whatever reasons — biological, cultural, or both — certain qualities have been viewed predominantly as feminine or masculine. In this regard, feminine has to do with openness, receptivity, and relationship. Masculine has to do with assertion, productivity, and individuality. Every person has a mixture of feminine and masculine qualities. Although most women face the world primarily with the feminine, they often also have unconscious masculine qualities. Most men ordinarily face the world with the masculine. But they also have feminine qualities within them. Persons move toward wholeness as they are able to recognize the feminine and masculine elements within themselves and to incorporate them into their lives. Both elements are equally valuable and critical in the journey toward human wholeness.

God already has this wholeness. As we have seen, the biblical writers used a variety of metaphors to emphasize that no words can "contain" God. God is beyond the gender descriptions of male and female. Yet God is revealed to us as one who has both feminine and masculine qualities. If we look at the metaphors we have explored thus far we can see that every one of them has both feminine and masculine elements.

That God is revealed as both assertive and receptive is seen in the final three metaphors you will be asked to explore: Word, Wisdom, and Spirit. These three metaphors are used often in the scriptures to describe how God is being revealed to God's people. In fact, one could easily spend at least six weeks using any one of them in prayer. I invite you now to explore these words in your prayer. Hopefully, in the process, they will help you to see the feminine and masculine elements within yourself, and enable you to become increasingly open *and* responsive to God and to others.

Reading: In openness to God, read Genesis 1:1–2:3.

Meditation: At first there was nothing but chaotic waters. "The earth was without form and void, and darkness was upon the face of the deep" (v 2a). But the Spirit of God was brooding over the face of the waters. And in God's own time, the Word was spoken . . . and creation began! Throughout this story we are told how God spoke forth the creation. Again and again we find these words: "And God said . . . and there was . . ."

The Word was spoken, and there was form! The firmament and the land with all its vegetation were brought into being where there had been void and emptiness.

The Word was spoken, and there was light! Out of the depths of darkness came the illumination of the sun, moon, and stars. The ordering of time and space was begun.

The Word was spoken, and there was life! Creatures populated the once empty land and air and sea. They swarmed and roamed and flew and swam. They multiplied, glorifying their Creator.

The Word was spoken, and humanity was created. In the image of God, men and women were brought to life in order to be companions with God and with each other.

They were created for the purpose of caring for the earth and all that is in it. On the last day God rested, looking over the creation. And God said, "It is good!"

This is a great story, this story of God "speaking forth" the creation. But it is not just an account written about events that took place long ago. The Word continues to be revealed in creation. God continues to speak forth order amid chaos and light amid darkness. God still creates living things to glorify their Creator. The Word continues to bring into being women and men to care for one another and for creation. The Word is not stagnant. God is always in the process of creating.

1.   Take some time now to be attentive to the gift of creation that God the Word has spoken into being. Go outside, either now or some time later today, and observe your surroundings. You may wish to go for a walk, using your senses of sight, hearing, smell, and touch to experience God's creation. Ask yourself this question, "What do I most appreciate about the world in which God has given me life?" Make notes about your experience.

2. Which word do you feel best describes humanity as we relate to the rest of creation: "consuming" or "caring"? What are the results of this relationship? Explain.

3. What can you as an individual do to be less consumptive and more caring in relation to the earth and its resources?

Response: Give thanks today for God's creative work. Confess your need to relate in more caring ways toward the earth. Ask God to help you to be a good steward of the gifts you have received.

During the day today observe the creation God continues to "speak forth."

Contemplation: As you end this time of prayer today, be sensitive to how the Word has been revealed to you.

Week 5, Day 2:

God the Word Becomes Flesh

Reading: Being still and open to the creative work God desires to do in you, read John 1:1–14.

Meditation: God never stops creating. The Word is always in the process of being revealed to us. This truth becomes clear as we turn to John 1. Notice all the images of creation in this passage. As God "spoke forth" the creation in the beginning, so God is continuing the process of creating by being revealed in Jesus Christ, "the Word [who] became flesh and dwelt among us." (v 14). Observe the images: "life" breathed into the lifeless (v 4), "light" breaking through the darkness (v 5), "identity" given to the nameless (v 12). In Jesus Christ, the Word made flesh, a "new creation" is being revealed!

1.   As you look at what John tells us about "the Word made flesh" in this passage, what do you learn about God?

2. Where do you see light in the world? Where do you
see darkness? Does it appear to you that the light is overcoming the darkness or is the darkness overcoming the
light? What are God's promises in regard to this?

The Word was revealed in a special way in Jesus
Christ. Words on a printed page can seem dry and lifeless.
But when they are "fleshed out," when someone speaks
them or orders their life by them, they come alive and
leave their mark upon all who are touched by them. Christ
lived out the way of peace and love, becoming the Word
for us. In Christ, God called all creation into more loving relationships with God's being and with others. In

response, we are invited to receive the Word and to become that Word for others. We are called to "flesh out" the
gospel of Christ in our everyday lives.

3. What does it mean for Christians to "flesh out" the
Word today?

4. How are you presently involved in making the Word
come alive for others?

Response: In your verbal prayers today, praise God for
the Word that has come alive in you through Christ. Ask
God to help you today to "flesh out" the Word for others.

During the day today be determined to live for Christ in your words and actions, that others may see the Word in you.

Contemplation: As you come to the end of this time of prayer, focus upon how God has been revealed to you today.

Week 5, Day 3

God the Word Nurtures Us

Reading: In the silence of your place of prayer, be open to God's presence. Then read Isaiah 55:6–13.

Meditation: The Word, which has been made alive in us in Christ, continues to do God's creative work in us. While the Word is revealed to us in many ways, one of the most important ways is through the scriptures. In the past several weeks, you have been asked to read a passage of scripture each day. Today, you are invited to consider further how you are receiving the Word through scripture.

In his book *Seeking the Face of God*, William H. Shannon reflects upon the use of the images of "rain and snow" to describe how the Word touches our lives. He suggests that there are at least two different types of rain. There is the brief rain that covers the surface of the ground very quickly, but never really penetrates the ground. This rain does little to make the ground fertile or fruitful. But there is also the long, gentle rain. This rain not only covers the surface, but goes deep into the soil. If the rain continues long enough, it saturates the ground, making it fertile and fruitful.[1]

1. Think now about the two types of rain described by Shannon. What insights can you gain from this about your reading of scripture? What kind of approach to the Bible is most beneficial? How well are you doing at this so far?

Shannon notes that this passage also likens the Word to snow. Like rain, snow nurtures the ground. But it does its work of watering in a different way. While rain tends to saturate the ground very quickly, snow usually falls on ground that has become hard and frozen. It may remain on the surface for a long time. But gradually the snow melts, and the water begins to penetrate to the depths of the soil.[2]

2.   The Word is revealed to us through the Bible. But
there are a variety of other ways God/Christ the Word
is revealed to us. List several of these ways in this space.

3.   Shannon notes that the frozen ground causes the nurturing water to remain on the surface for a long time before it finally can penetrate into the soil. What do you see
in your life that may be inhibiting the Word from pene-
trating more deeply into your life?

Consider now the promise of this text in verse 11: the
Word "shall accomplish that which I purpose, and prosper
in the thing for which I sent it."

4.   In what way do you feel the Word is nurturing you at
the present time? How are God's purposes for you being
accomplished?

Response: In your verbal prayers today, give thanks to God for the ways God has been revealed to you in the past and is being revealed to you in the present. Ask God to help you to be receptive to the Word that may be spoken to you today.

During the day today, consider the images of rain and snow that Isaiah uses in verse 10. Think about what they reveal to you about your own life in God.

Contemplation: In silence, be open to how God has been moving in your life during your prayer time today.

Week 5, Day 4:

God, the Word, Confronts Us

Reading: Having returned to your familiar place of prayer, rest in silence for a while. Then read Hebrews 4:11–13.

Meditation: Even though they may be faced with many struggles in their lives, people of faith often find that they feel a sense of peace and contentment within themselves as they become more and more attentive to God. The

Word nurtures us as we gradually absorb the refreshing presence of God into our lives. But, as our reading for today reminds us, the Word also challenges us. There is always this feeling that we have not yet "arrived" when we are open to the Word. When we are in Christ, we are always in the process of becoming "new creations."

The Word is described in this passage as confrontive. It is "living and active" (v 12). It is "piercing," "sharper than any two-edged sword" (v 12). And it is "discerning," bringing to light the thoughts and intentions of the heart, laying bare that which is hidden (v 12–13). As the Word is revealed to us, we begin to see ourselves as we really are. Surely God looks at the "new creation" we are becoming and says, "It is good!" But God also observes what is not yet redeemed in us, and confronts us with it. It can be disconcerting indeed to be "pierced" by the truth of God's Word.

1.   As you think about your life at the present time, can you identify some area in you that needs redemption? Is there some way that you have been unloving in your relationships with God, your neighbors, or yourself? Being as specific as you can, write about that.

One of the most helpful things about keeping a written record of our reflections during prayer is that we can return to them and see what God has done in us in the past. Often, without writing, we may lose sight of some important truth that God has revealed to us in our prayer. Turn now to page 28 of this workbook, and answer the following questions.

2.   On that day, as you used Luke 15:11–19 to explore how God, the Father, gives us freedom to fail, you were asked to identify your sin in question #1. How does your answer to that question compare with your answer to the first question in today's prayer experience?

3.   Observe what progress you have made in relating more lovingly to God, your neighbor, and yourself during these last several weeks. Make some notes about that here.

4. What do you feel the Word is calling you to do to become still more loving?

Response: In your prayers today be aware of what God
has revealed to you about yourself and your relationships
with God and with others. Confess your sins to God, and
ask God to help you to be open to the Word's redemptive
work in you.

During the day, recall these words: "Therefore, if anyone is in Christ, he [or she] is a new creation; the old has
passed away, behold, the new has come" (2 Cor 5:17).

Contemplation: In silence, be attentive to what God has
revealed to you during your prayer time today.

Week 5, Day 5:

God Is Revealed as Wisdom

Reading: Following a time of silence, read Proverbs 1:20–33.

Meditation: In his book *The Way of the Heart*, Henri J.M. Nouwen suggests that people in our society today have "compulsive" lifestyles. He writes:

> Just look for a moment at our daily routine. In general we are very busy people.... Our calendars are filled with appointments, our days and weeks filled with engagements, and our years filled with plans and projects. There is seldom a period in which we do not know what to do, and we move through life in such a distracted way that we do not even take the time and rest to wonder if any of the things we think, say, or do are worth thinking, saying, or doing. We simply go along with the many "musts" and "oughts" that have been handed on to us, and we live with them as if they were authentic translations of the gospel of our Lord.[3]

Notice, as you read the text from Proverbs, the contrast between the way of the "simple" and the way of Wisdom. Wisdom is ever seeking to reveal to us her way. She desires to offer us the guidance that would make our thoughts, words, and actions express the true purposes of God (v 23). But we live in a world where the tendency is to choose the way of the "simple." It is easy to get caught up in the compulsiveness of doing many things so that we are not open to God, whose Wisdom would be revealed to us (v 24–25). Getting caught up in their own "devices," no matter how pure they may seem, the "simple" fail to heed the "counsel" and "reproof" of Wisdom (v 30–31).

1.   As you look at the world around you, can you give some examples of the compulsiveness that Nouwen writes about? What are the consequences of this constant distraction?

2.   Where do you see compulsiveness in your own life? In what ways have you chosen the way of the "simple"?

3. How do you hear Wisdom calling out to you at the present time? What would Wisdom say to you that you most need in life right now?

Response: In your verbal prayers today confess your own compulsiveness. Ask God to help you to seek the way of Wisdom, rather than to adopt the way of the "simple." Pray for those who you feel are suffering from their own compulsiveness.

During the day today observe your lifestyle. Consider what you could do to allow more time and space for receiving Wisdom.

Contemplation: In silence, be attentive to what God has revealed to you during your prayer time. Observe what meaning your thoughts, words, and actions have at this time for your life.

Week 5, Day 6:

The Way of Wisdom

Reading: Remember that spiritual reading is done slowly, as if we are taking in some favorite food. After you have become still in your place of prayer, read Proverbs 2:1–15.

Meditation: We are always making decisions in life. Some are routine, requiring little thought. Others are a little more difficult. They demand more of our attention and have more of an influence upon our lives or the lives of others. Still others are major decisions. They call forth great energy from us because the direction we choose could affect our lives or the lives of others for years to come.

1.   Think about a major decision you either have made or are in the process of making at the present time. What is involved in that decision?

As we observed yesterday, it is difficult for people caught up in compulsiveness to be aware of the meaning of their thoughts, words, or deeds. It is important, if we are to be open to the guidance of Wisdom, to set apart times such as this for prayer and meditation. Regular prayer time can be helpful to us as we make the routine decisions of everyday life. It can be pivotal for us when we are in the midst of making major decisions. For it is at these times that we most need the direction of God, our Wisdom.

Notice as you consider this passage what difference it makes to be open to Wisdom. Those who are guided by Wisdom are described as people who receive "knowledge and understanding" (v 5–6). They have "integrity," and understand "righteousness" and "justice" and "equity" (v 7–9). Their lives are so shaped by the presence of God that they use careful "discretion" in making decisions and are delivered from the way of evil (v 10–12).

2.   Our faith gives us several resources which help us to be open to the influence of Wisdom. In this workbook we have used the resources of scripture, prayer, and journaling. Where else might you turn to find Wisdom when you have important decisions to make?

3.   As you think about the description in Proverbs 2 of a person who is influenced by Wisdom, how may your use of the resources of our faith affect decisions you have to make? What does it mean to make decisions with integrity, or to be conscious of righteousness, justice, and equity in making decisions?

Response: Give thanks to God for providing resources for you to use in receiving Wisdom in making decisions. Pray for decisions you have to make, being conscious of how those decisions may affect your relationship with God, others, and yourself.

During the day today, give some thought to the decision you described in question #1 above. How might Wisdom influence that decision?

Contemplation: As you end this time in silence, observe what you have received from God in your prayer today.

Week 5, Day 7:

Summary, Week 5

Reading: Review your daily workbook experiences. Read with an openness to what you see revealed in these pages.

Meditation: The following questions may help to guide your reflections about your prayer experiences this week:

1.   What are the most important things you discovered about God during this week?

2. What did you learn about yourself as you explored these metaphors?

3. Can you identify some of your feelings during this week?

4. Is there anything you feel called to do as a result of
your reflections this week? If so, what will you need to do
to respond to this calling?

5. What questions or concerns do you have that relate to
your experience of this week?

Response: Offer to God whatever prayers seem to respond to your experience of this week.

Contemplation: In silence, be aware of what has been revealed to you during your prayer time today.

Notes

1 William H. Shannon, *Seeking the Face of God* (New York: Crossroad, 1988), p. 42.

2 Ibid., p. 43.

3 Henri J.M. Nouwen, *The Way of the Heart* (New York: Ballantine Books, 1981), p. 10.

WEEK SIX

Metaphors of
Wisdom and Spirit

Week 6, Day 1:

Wisdom Amid Suffering

Reading: Spend a few moments becoming attentive to God. Then read Job 28:12–28.

Meditation: "Why do the innocent suffer?" Job's query is one of the most pressing of all human questions. You remember how Job was afflicted. Everything he had — his possessions, his family, his health — was taken away. In the midst of his struggle he searched for some reason why he suffered. He felt that if he could find the answer to that question, then somehow his condition would be easier to deal with.

Much of the book of Job is a search for the wisdom to know why he suffered. He consults with his wife and his friends, but their rationalizations only cause him to feel more guilty and angry about his plight. Even in his conversations with God, Job does not find an answer to his question. However, in his journey to discover the reason for suffering, Job receives an important truth. He finds that God alone understands his suffering. And he sees that true peace will come for him not in finding some reason to explain his predicament, but in relationship with God. In God, who is present with him in the midst of all of life, including its turmoil, Job can find the strength and the wisdom to sustain him. God reveals this truth to Job: "Behold, the fear of the Lord, that is wisdom; and to depart from evil is understanding" (v. 28).

1.   As you look around you in the world, where do you
see innocent suffering?

2.   Where do you see suffering in your own life and in
the lives of others in your family and among your friends?

3.   As you think about your own suffering and the suffering of others, where do you see God being revealed
in it?

4.   What difference does it make for you that God is
present amid suffering even though the suffering itself
may not end?

Response: As you express your prayers today, give thanks
for God's presence amid your suffering. Pray for those

who suffer in your family and in the world. Be open to the wisdom God would give you in the face of their suffering and your own.

During the day, meditate upon this verse: "I consider that the sufferings of this present time are not worth comparing with the glory that is to be revealed to us" (Rom 8:18).

Contemplation: Be attentive now to how God has been present with you during your time of prayer.

Week 6, Day 2:

Jesus Christ, the Wisdom of God

Reading: Being open to what God, the true Wisdom, would reveal to you, read I Corinthians 1:18–25.

Meditation: "The word of the cross is folly to those who are perishing, but to us who are being saved it is the power of God" (v 18). To a world enamored with displays of power, with might and wealth and celebrity, it doesn't make sense that the Christ would die as a criminal on a cross. In an age when being competent, well-educated, and financially successful is highly valued, it seems shocking that the Chosen One of God should be found crucified among the least and the lost. The Jews were looking for signs of power. They expected a mighty king to redeem them from their oppression. The Greeks were impressed by intellect. They would have responded better to a messiah who could display some physical proof of being the Holy One of God. On the basis of the "wisdom of this world," as the apostle Paul describes it here, the cross of Christ seems like foolishness.

1.   What do you see as the consequences of life today
when lived according to the "wisdom of this world"?

The cross of Christ seems like folly on the basis of
human wisdom. But, says Paul, "Christ is the power of
God and the wisdom of God" (v 24).

2.   What does the Christ who was crucified upon a cross
reveal to you about Wisdom?

3. What sort of power would be displayed in the life of one who lived the way of God's Wisdom in Christ?

4. What would you need to do in your life in order to live the way of Christ crucified?

Response: Give thanks for the gift of God in Jesus Christ. Confess how the cross of Christ is a stumbling block for you. Ask God to help you live the way of the cross.

During the day, repeat Paul's words: "To us who are being saved, [the Cross] is the [wisdom] and power of God."

Contemplation: Close your time of prayer as you began it, being open to what God would reveal to you in the silence.

Week 6, Day 3:

God the Spirit Enables Us to Move Toward Wholeness

Reading: Following your time of stillness, read Ezekiel 37:1–14.

Meditation: Throughout the Old Testament we find God's people identifying God's presence among them as the Spirit or "breath" of God. In Genesis 2:7, for example, we find God breathing life into humanity, so that women and men became living beings. Here, in Ezekiel 37, we see God's Spirit coming as "wind" to breathe life into a lifeless people.

The people of God are described in this text as "dry bones." Because they had turned from God, the people of Israel had been taken into exile by a foreign oppressor. In a strange land, they were without hope, fearing that their life as a community would never again be restored.

1.   Try to identify your own brokenness as an individual. Perhaps it is something small compared to the great tragedy of God's people long ago. What is it that makes you feel anxious or afraid or distant from God at the present time?

2.   As you look at the life of your community of faith,
is there any place you see "dry bones," or the need for
restoration? Describe it.

   To the troubled people of Israel, God proclaimed a
word of promise: "Behold, I will cause breath to enter you
and you shall live" (v 5). God the Spirit would be revealed
to them, and there would be living flesh where once there
had been dry bones. In the midst of their brokenness, God

would bring wholeness. While they presently were hope-lessly scattered, they would once again become a commu-nity of faith who would celebrate life under the reign of God.

3.   How do you see the Spirit of God restoring your bro-kenness, moving you toward wholeness? What are the signs of God's breath filling you?

4.   In what ways do you see the Spirit moving in your church? What evidence of God's presence is there in that fellowship?

5. As a result of your meditations upon how God's Spirit is working in you and in your church, what do you feel called to do?

Response: In openness to the restoring work of God in your life and in your church, make these words your prayer for today:

> Breathe on me, Breath of God,
> Fill me with life anew,
> That I may love what Thou dost love,
> And do what Thou wouldst do.
> — Edwin Hatch

During the day today focus upon what it would mean for you to be so influenced by the breath of God that you would love as God loves.

Contemplation: In silence, be sensitive to how God has been moving in you during your time of prayer.

Week 6, Day 4:

God the Spirit Empowers Us

Reading: Begin in silence. Then read Luke 4:16–21.

Meditation: In the power of the Spirit, Jesus had just spent forty days in the wilderness. Now, as he began his ministry, he "returned in the power of the Spirit" to his hometown of Nazareth. In the synagogue he was invited to read from the prophet Isaiah. Surely the passage he chose to read would be good news for some but bad news for others. With joy the weak of his day would receive these words about "good news to the poor" and "release to the captives." They would gladly hear the message of "recovery of sight to the blind," and of "liberty for the oppressed." But for those in power who were comfortable with things as they were in spite of all the injustices, this was a piercing sermon. For Jesus was talking about a reordering of life as they knew it.

1.   Recall a time when you became especially aware of Christ's presence in your life. Perhaps Christ came to you in the form of some good news that enriched your life. Or maybe during a difficult time you received "release" and felt "set free" from your burdens. Or perhaps he helped you to see something about yourself or your world more clearly and it was as if you "recovered your sight." Write about your experience here, explaining what it was like for you. Include how your life was changed as a result of that experience.

Through the Holy Spirit, Christ continues to be revealed to us, offering us salvation. But that same Spirit of God that empowered Christ to be in ministry also calls us to love and serve others. In a unique way Christ was anointed by the Spirit at his baptism as the Chosen One of God. But we also have been anointed at our baptisms to continue the ministry of Christ in the world.

2.   Who are the poor, the captives, the blind, and the oppressed at the present time? Be as specific as you can in identifying them.

3.   What do you see as your ministry to them? What do you need to do to fulfill that ministry?

4.   In I Corinthians 12 Paul talks about the "gifts of the Spirit." What gifts has the Spirit given you to enable you to participate in Christ's ministry to the world?

Response: Praise God for the presence of the Spirit in your life. Pray for those who are poor, held captive, blind, and oppressed. Ask God to help you to identify ways that you can best fulfill your ministry at the present time.

During the day, do some act of service for someone you have identified in question #2 above.

Contemplation: Be silent and open to what God has revealed to you today.

Week 6, Day 5:

God the Spirit Counsels Us

Reading: Having returned to your place of prayer, know that God's Spirit is present with you. Read John 16:7–11.

Meditation: Jesus promised his disciples that they would not be alone following his death, resurrection, and ascension. He would send them a "Counselor," or a caring friend, to be with them. So far we have seen how the Spirit acts powerfully, breathing life into the lifeless and empowering God's people for ministry. Today I invite you to consider that God's Spirit also relates to us gently, listening and caring for us, guiding us into relationship with God.

1.   Most of us have the privilege in life of relating to a trusted friend. Think about someone who has been a counselor for you. You may think of a professional who has been especially helpful, if you have had that kind of relationship. Or a close friend or family member who listens and cares may come to mind. Describe your relationship with that person. Consider what it is that makes his or her friendship so valuable to you.

2.   Keeping in mind your description of that relationship, what does it mean to say God is a counselor?

3.   Notice that the disciples were troubled at the thought of Jesus' departure from them. It is perhaps when we are troubled in life that we most need that trusted friend. How have you experienced God's Spirit as a caring friend amid your troubles?

4. Consider now that the Counselor not only was to listen to the disciples in their troubles, but also to guide
them concerning "sin," "righteousness," and "judgment"
(v 8–9). As you consider your experiences of prayer this
week, where do you most clearly see the Spirit guiding
you?

Response: As you pray today, speak to God whatever may
be troubling you at the present time about yourself or
about others. Know that your Counselor is present to listen to you. Pray for the Spirit to guide you as you continue through this day.

During the day today, focus upon these words:

Come, Holy Spirit, fill the hearts
    of your faithful
and kindle in them the fire of
    your love.
Send forth your Spirit, O Lord,
    and renew the face of the earth.

Contemplation: Be open to the presence of the Spirit, who
desires to be your dearest friend.

Week 6, Day 6:

Life in the Spirit

Reading: In this place of prayer that has become "home" for you by now, read Galatians 5:16–26.

Meditation: The apostle Paul draws a striking contrast in this text between two ways of life. One is "life according to the flesh." The other is "life in the Spirit." Spend some time now putting into your own words Paul's description of these two ways of life.

1.   "Life according to the flesh" is . . .

2.   "Life in the Spirit" is . . .

3.   What evidence do you see in your own life at the present time that you continue to live "according to the flesh"?

4.   What evidence do you see in yourself of "life in the Spirit"?

Prayer plays an important part in enabling us to bear the "fruit of the Spirit." You have arrived now at the next to the last day of this journey of prayer. Hopefully you will continue to keep the discipline of setting apart a time and place for prayer in your daily life. One of the purposes of this workbook was to invite you to experience a style of prayer you may wish to use on your own. There are a variety of ways you can find material for *lectio divina*. You could spend several days or weeks exploring further each of the metaphors suggested in this book. Or you could "work through" a larger portion of scripture over a period of time following the four stages you used here. Or you may start with a daily devotional booklet, reading the suggested scripture lesson, and allowing the readings to be a springboard for your own meditation and response. The important thing is that you continue on the journey of growing in your awareness of God's presence in your life and responding in loving ways to God, your neighbors, and yourself.

Response: In your prayer today, be open to the leading of the Spirit as you consider your continuing journey of prayer. Following your prayer, you may wish to write a covenant statement, committing yourself to a particular discipline of prayer for a certain period of time. Give thanks to God for how God has been revealed to you. Pray for the grace to continue to be faithful in your prayer life.

Contemplation: End your prayer time today as you have ended it each day: in silence. Be open to what God has revealed to you during this time of prayer.

Week 6, Day 7:

Summary, Week 6

Reading: Review your daily workbook experiences for this week. Read with an openness to what you see revealed in these pages.

Meditation: The following questions may help to guide your reflections about your prayer experiences:

1. What are the most important things you discovered about God during this week?

2. What did you learn about yourself as you explored these metaphors?

3. Can you identify some of your feelings during this week?

4. Is there anything you feel called to do as a result of your reflections this week? If so, what will you need to do to respond to this calling?

5.   What questions or concerns do you have that relate to your experience this week?

Response: Offer to God whatever prayers seem to respond to your experience of this week.

Contemplation: In silence, be aware of what has been revealed to you during your prayer time today.

Reference List

While the daily devotional guides used in this workbook have grown out of my own use of biblical metaphors in prayer, several resources were helpful to me in directing me to scripture texts related to the various metaphors for God. Readers may wish to refer to these resources as they continue to use metaphors for God in their own prayer lives.

Butterick, George Arthur, ed. *The Interpreter's Dictionary of the Bible* (Nashville: Abingdon Press, 1962). See especially the following articles:

_____. "God, Names of," by Bernard W. Anderson.

_____. "God, OT view of," by Bernard W. Anderson.

_____. "God, NT view of," by C.F.D. Moule.

Crim, Keith, ed. *The Interpreter's Dictionary of the Bible, Supplementary Volume* (Nashville: Abingdon Press, 1976). See especially "God, Nature of, in the OT," by Phyllis Trible.

Hardesty, Nancy A. *Inclusive Language in the Church* (Atlanta: John Knox Press, 1987).

Leech, Kenneth. *Experiencing God: Theology as Spirituality* (San Francisco: Harper and Row, Publishers, 1985).

Mollenkott, Virginia Ramey. *The Divine Feminine: The Biblical Imagery of God as Female* (New York: Crossroad, 1986).

Morrison, Clinton, ed. *An Analytical Concordance of the Revised Standard Version of the New Testament* (Philadelphia: The Westminster Press, 1979).

Mulholland, M. Robert, Jr. *Shaped by the Word: The Power of Scripture in Spiritual Formation* (Nashville: The Upper Room, 1985).

Strong, James, ed. *Strong's Exhaustive Concordance of the Bible*, 32 ed. (Nashville: Abingdon, 1974).

Swidler, Leonard. *Biblical Affirmations of Woman* (Philadelphia: Westminster Press, 1979).